Praise for *The Activation Imperative*

"*The Activation Imperative* offers readers a practical approach to the transformation needed to respond to today's accelerating pace of technological change. It is as valuable to today's marketing practitioners as it is to academics. A must read for anyone interested in increasing the effectiveness of modern marketing."
—**Yoram (Jerry) Wind, Lauder Professor Emeritus of Marketing, Wharton School, University of Pennsylvania**

"*The Activation Imperative* is an essential read for any marketer hoping to stay relevant in a rapidly changing marketplace. Rosen and Minsky build a compelling argument for moving beyond carpet-bombing prospective customers with brand promotion to engaging them at key trigger points in the customer journey. With its keen insights on building both brand and bottom-line results, this is one book you don't want to miss!"
—**Rick Mathieson, author of *Branding Unbound* and *The On-Demand Brand***

"Rosen and Minsky have written a must-read primer for marketing professionals. Anyone who aspires to master versatile and creative tactical marketing strategies and the strategic framework of thinking in a customer-centric and ever-changing marketplace should read this book."
—**Jenna Massey, Medill School of Journalism, Media, Integrated Marketing Communications, Northwestern University**

"In our recent groundbreaking study, the Association of National Advertisers found that spending on brand activation will top $740 billion by 2020, more than twice as much as advertising. I'm glad to finally see a book like *The Activation Imperative* that is not only focused on brand activation but also provides a methodology for better aligning marketing disciplines to achieve it."
—**Michael P. Kaufman, senior vice president of brand activation, Association of National Advertisers**

The Activation Imperative

How to Build Brands and Business by Inspiring Action

William Rosen and
Laurence Minsky

Foreword by Rory Sutherland

ROWMAN & LITTLEFIELD
Lanham • Boulder • New York • London

Published by Rowman & Littlefield
A wholly owned subsidary of The Rowman & Littlefield Publishing Group, Inc.
4501 Forbes Boulevard, Suite 200, Lanham, Maryland 20706
www.rowman.com

Unit A, Whitacre Mews, 26-34 Stannary Street, London SE11 4AB, United Kingdom

British Library Cataloguing in Publication Information Available

Library of Congress Cataloging-in-Publication Data Available

ISBN 978-1-4422-5704-7 (cloth : alk.paper)
ISBN 978-1-5381-1466-7 (pbk. : alk. paper)
ISBN 978-1-4422-5705-4 (electronic)

♾™ The paper used in this publication meets the minimum requirements of American National Standard for Information Sciences—Permanence of Paper for Printed Library Materials, ANSI/NISO Z39.48-1992.

Printed in the United States of America

To Carole, Hayden, and Ariyel,
whose love and support make everything possible.

—W. R.

To the memories of Stephen R. Cartozian and James Lucas—
each a friend, mentor, and
unrelenting marketing innovator

—L. M.

Contents

Acknowledgments

Special thanks to David Aron, Jane Berliss-Vincent, Adam Brown, Matt Carlson, Courtney Cashman, Nicholas Cavet, Heidi Clyde, Colleen Fahey, Stevie Fitzgerald, Edna Guerra, Dr. Charles Hammerslough, Carli Hansen, Julie Harris, Patrick Herron, Brian Hodes, David Houle, Rodrigo Hurtado, Andrea O. Kendrick, Kwang-Ku Kim, Hannah Kinisky, James Lucas, Erin Lynch, Suzanne McBride, Suzanne McGee, Alton Miller, Ann Marie Mitchell, Margaret Murphy, Patrick Palmer, Alden Perkins, Rachel Ready, Christopher Richert, Raymond P. Schmitz Jr., Craig Sigele, Leanne Silverman, Karie Simpson, Sarah Stanton, Claudia Strauss, Leonard Strazewski, Rory Sutherland, Carol Timberlake, Sarah Vonderhaar, Morgan Waller, Stanley Wearden, Natalie Wilkinson, Pam Workman, and, of course, our families, the blind peer reviewers (whom we will never meet, but who helped to shape the content in ways they will never know through their feedback on our proposal and manuscript), and the baristas who kept us caffeinated.

Foreword

RORY SUTHERLAND, VICE CHAIRMAN, OGILVY &
MATHER GROUP UK

*"Because the purpose of business is to create a customer, the business enterprise has two—
and only two—basic functions: marketing and innovation. Marketing and innovation
produce results; all the rest are costs."*

It's a famous quotation. But I think Peter Drucker here misses one important
final conceptual leap. Which is that, when you define them properly, marketing and innovation are often the same thing. Or, at the very least, two sides
of the same coin.

Economic value is very largely created by innovation: when people newly
discover the means to do desirable and worthwhile things that they previously
could not do.

But changing habits and norms of behavior is as much a marketing challenge as it is a technological one. At the very simplest level, there is no point
in building a new road or railway line if no one knows of its existence. But
similarly there is no point in creating better technologies until people have
the confidence to adopt them. Plenty of good ideas have failed—or been very
slow to take hold—because of psychological factors.

(I have long argued, for instance, that videoconferencing has largely failed
to supplant physical travel because it was badly marketed—being sold as a
poor man's alternative to air travel rather than as a rich man's version of the
phone call.)

As an Austrian, Drucker (both he and his economist father were friends with Joseph Schumpeter) knew this already. The Austrian School of Economics has always been clear that "value" is subjective. And hence—almost alone among economic modes of thought—it has been very accepting of the value of marketing. As Schumpeter's intellectual ancestor Ludwig von Mises remarked, "There is no sensible distinction between the value created in a restaurant by the man who cooks the food and the man who sweeps the floor." He is using the floor-sweeper here as an analogy for marketing and advertising. Just as there is a value to producing the food, there is also a value to creating an environment in which the food can be enjoyed to its utmost. There is no point in producing excellent meals in a restaurant that smells of sewage, just as there is no point in creating stunning technological advances if you lack the skills to encourage people confidently to adopt them. (I worry, for instance, there are still no widely recognized brands of solar panels.)

Two years ago, Stewart Butterfield, a Silicon Valley innovator and one of the cofounders of both Flickr and Slack, made the following comment in an email to his colleagues: "The best—maybe the only?—real, direct measure of 'innovation' is change in human behavior. In fact, it is useful to take this way of thinking as definitional: innovation is the sum of change across the whole system, not a thing which causes a change in how people behave. No small innovation ever caused a large shift in how people spend their time and no large one has ever failed to do so."

I think Butterfield is almost certainly right here. And, seen through this lens, marketing and innovation are simply two complementary means of achieving the same end: to provide people with the technological and psychological cues through which they can satisfy new desires. Whether you achieve this by creating new products or by creating new desires (or both) is an irrelevant distinction.

As William and Laurence kindly acknowledge in this book, I have always believed that the best way to approach marketing challenges is by adopting a behavior-first approach. Start by being absolutely clear about what final behavior you wish to see, and then work backward from that point, experimenting and optimizing as you go. (In shopper marketing this approach is sometimes called "Shelf-back planning.")

Starting with the end point and then working backward makes obvious sense to me. There is no point in optimizing upstream when bottlenecks or inefficiencies still persist downstream. By contrast, if you make your website conversion twice as effective, then any advertising you subsequently run will be made twice as effective as a result.

I am also a huge fan of defining success in behavioral terms—whether the behavior is a sale or, in the case of social marketing, a new habit or norm.

To borrow the language of genetics, behavior is dominant; attitude is recessive. As Adam Ferrier observes below, when people adopt a behavior, their attitudes tend subsequently to fall into line; this is less true the other way round. A focus on behavior also allows you to quantify the value of success—and thus decide how much to spend—in a way in which intermediate metrics such as attitude and awareness don't.

But there is an even bigger reason why all marketing agencies should support behavioral metrics. And it is something we have increasingly discovered at Ogilvy & Mather since requiring that all briefs are headed by a clear behavioral objective.

First of all, defining success in behavioral terms broadens the scope of discussion. Rather than getting trapped in a very narrow brand debate, talk of behavior fosters a broad-ranging discussion of the market as a complex system—which markets undoubtedly are. Does the price need to change? The payment terms? Would it make a difference if we accepted contactless payments? Where are the moments on customer journeys in which interventions will have the most effect? What is the necessary balance of encouragement versus reassurance? Do people need to hear of the product from a trusted authority or via their friends? Should we establish new distribution channels?

This conversation is creatively liberating to an extraordinary degree. To a man with only a hammer, everything looks like a nail. But, equally, to a man with only a bag of nails, every tool looks like a hammer.

If you focus only on attitudinal objectives, say, every different agency and skillset is essentially competing to do the same job. However, when you look at a problem through the lens of behavior—considering the many different drivers of behavior and the different roles different forms of communication may play at different stages of the journey—well, then, the collaboration and cooperation the authors speak of in their opening chapter comes about automatically.

Then the question becomes, "How can all of our skills complement each other best to create the desired end behavior?" This is always a better approach, but as this book makes wonderfully clear, its superiority becomes even more apparent in the fragmented and diverse media environment we now inhabit.

Perhaps most important of all, the consumer benefits too. One of the problems of using all marketing communications to change everyone's underlying attitude is that it leads to a very noisy world. At every turn, the target audience are bombarded with conflicting messages from competing brands. In every medium, at every opportunity, people are trying to change my mind. This at some point becomes intolerable. Even if it pays to do this at an individual level, it makes the whole system worse and will lead to ad-blocking and general disengagement.

One of the great advantages of this new approach, by contrast, is that it not only tells us when to talk, and how to do so with relevance, but also tells us when to shut up. Given the percentage of our days now devoted to media consumption, that may be the greatest benefit of all.

Preface

At a time of unprecedented innovation and opportunity in the world of marketing, it remains remarkable how much discussion and attention is focused on subjects other than effectiveness.

The two of us had the good fortune (or misfortune, depending on perspective) to come of age as marketers in an environment and working with brands that were explicitly focused on delivering the most effective marketing solutions possible, as defined by maximum performance against business results at minimum cost. Any and all types of innovative ideas, media channels, creative elements, and tactical tools that were legal, ethical, and on brand were not only accepted, but expected by the brand marketing leaders who would be evaluating, testing, implementing, and measuring those deemed worthy.

The blessing of an unrelenting and unwavering focus on effectiveness is that it opens one's mind to the full range of possible ways to achieve it. It compels one to not only understand every aspect of the brand and business in an effort to discover the limits of what is operationally and authentically feasible, but also to search for every potential lever that can be pulled to more cost-effectively drive and improve market results, be they strategic partnerships, new product offerings, untapped audiences, or unexpected points of contact.

It also leads one to quickly realize that when the preeminent goal is effectiveness, one of the most powerful tools available to the brand and marketer is strategic collaboration.

Since the first multicell organism formed from several single-cell organ-isms utilizing the power of their cross-functional synergies to survive and thrive, to the social contract of mutually agreed-upon rights and responsibili-ties that are the foundation of every civilized society, strategic collaboration has been one of the keys to improving the effective achievement of goals in the world at large, as well as in the world of marketing.

During this extended period of ever-increasing specialization, driven by well-chronicled technical innovation and media fragmentation, those of us who have had the privilege and opportunity to actually functionally connect groups of specialized companies and subject-matter experts have learned how to do so to not only be measurably more effective than traditional integrated marketing communications (IMC) approaches, but also to, in fact, utilize the best practices from each to improve the effectiveness of the others. Over time, and with repeated applications and measurement, one begins to identify core methodologies and approaches that are more effective than others, and discover how to scale those approaches by structuring organizations around them and teaching their application to others.

That is the reason we wrote this book.

We wanted to shift the discussion, from inspirations and aspirations of what we all know we want to achieve, to *applications* capable of actually achieving them.

From debates over the relative merits of disciplines, to methodologies that utilize them collectively and synergistically to maximum effect.

From positioning data science in opposition to creativity, to demonstrat-ing how they can be more powerful and effective together.

From an ongoing tension between brand building and business building, to delivering both to the benefit of each.

When one unrelentingly focuses on effectiveness, one realizes that while attitudes, awareness, intentions, and beliefs are all critical, behaviors are everything. Because with the behaviors of people and brands at the center, creative ideas can become powerful vehicles of change, collaboration can be fuel, measurement is not an option, and the best solutions, by definition, work the best.

We are in a time of unprecedented opportunity and unmatched expec-tations—where those focused on effectiveness and return on investment (ROI) are driving fragmentation into convergence. Those of us who have the good fortune to work strategically, creatively, and technically across these specialized worlds can share what we have learned to help others unite them, apply them, scale them, and teach them to others.

The Activation Imperative began as an online article originally published by the *Harvard Business Review* as part of the HBR Insight Center "Marketing That Works" series. We were honored and gratified that our approach was selected for inclusion—even if it did leave us curious as to what categories existed outside of "Marketing That Works," and extremely grateful to have not been placed among them.

In this expansion and deeper explication of the concepts outlined in our original article, we have a lot to share. But before you begin reading, we want to ask one favor: Please promise us that you will simply try the Activation Imperative Method on a select marketing challenge, measure the results, and share them with us and our readers via our website at activationimperative .com. We promise that you will be glad you did.

Now, enjoy, and onward.

1

AIM for Greater ROI

The Activation Imperative Method

In the early 2000s, a powerful confluence of challenging economic conditions and emerging digital platforms began to drive a substantial shift in the marketing world. While the economic environment forced marketing decision makers to increase their focus on return on investment (ROI), digital platforms from social media to mobile started enabling more personalized and trackable marketing communications.[1]

In the years since, the demand for continual improvements in marketing return has become the new normal—and the ability to track and personalize interactions has only continued to increase.[2]

To thrive in this changed landscape, marketers need to shift from merely building brands to fully activating them—from simply projecting what a brand *is* to optimizing what a brand *does* in order to reach the right people in the right way to change their behavior and move them closer to a transaction.

This is the Activation Imperative.

Much of traditional marketing has concentrated on the positioning of a brand relative to its competitors—identifying space the brand owns in the marketplace that is clearly differentiated from that of competitive brands. In these brand-building efforts, the emphasis is on articulating what the brand is and stands for, and what the marketer ultimately wants it to mean to the consumer. The messaging focus is on communicating the essence of the brand via features, benefits, and unique selling propositions, with the assumption that if repeated with sufficient frequency, these awareness-driving activities would over time be enough to drive sales.

Developing this type of clear, differentiated brand foundation is still absolutely critical. Marketers need to know with great precision where their brand fits in the marketplace, and where they intend it to live in the hearts and minds of their target consumers. Marketers must define what the brand is, clarify what it stands for, and determine how its essence will be artfully and consistently expressed in all relevant contexts to maximize its appeal to its target market. While today's consumers are playing a larger and more active role in defining brand meaning[3] (a role many would say consumers have always played, albeit less visibly), marketers cannot abdicate their responsibility for communicating with intention and providing consumers with the tools, cues, and information they need to understand and value the brand. There is, after all, no doubt that when effectively established, strong brands can command a premium versus competitors,[4] are better able to weather the occasional storms of product issues or shifts in market dynamics,[5] and can more easily expand into related products or categories.[6]

However, this type of brand building, while absolutely necessary, is no longer *sufficient*.

To drive trial of new products, increase visits to a retailer's store or site, fuel trade-up to higher-end products, increase purchase frequency, or propel greater sharing and advocacy, marketers need to activate specific *behaviors* by their consumers while building the brand.

By understanding that the challenge—and the opportunity—is about behaviors, and, more specifically, behavior *change*, the need to consider and utilize a wider range of tools, tactics, channels, and approaches beyond simply creating awareness becomes clear. What becomes equally clear is the need to understand what consumers (or shoppers) are doing when and why in order to enable marketers to create relevant and welcome opportunities for engagement. When those opportunities are identified and seized in a truly branded way, the marketer can reap the benefit of creating engagement with the brand that not only helps to advance the consumer toward transaction, but also demonstrates the brand's essence and values through meaningful and memorable actions and interactions that set the stage for future activations.

LIVING IN COMPLEX TIMES

Fortunately, today's marketer has a robust suite of marketing tools and opportunities to drive engagement beyond simply trumpeting the brand essence. Mobile invitations to unique experiences, socially shared interactive videos, digitally delivered content, and in-store events are but a few. These increased opportunities, however, have also created increased complexity for the marketer.

The unique strategic, creative, and technological skills, insights, processes, and people required by state-of-the-art digital, social, mobile, database, sponsorship, and shopper marketing have driven increased specialization. Each area requires its own constantly up-to-date expertise in the latest technical innovations, strategic shifts, and tactical opportunities. As a result, it makes complete sense why the partner or department that is clear on the implications of an algorithm change in a major social media platform may not be aware of a shift in the priorities of a key retail partner, the latest techniques in predictively modeling behavior, or the newest sponsorship opportunities.

Long gone are the days when chief marketing officers (CMOs) or marketing departments only needed to manage a standard set of three partners: an advertising agency, a public relations firm, and a marketing services agency that handled all of the "below the line" efforts from direct to retail marketing. Now, with the rapid growth of specialized services and fragmenting markets, marketers can be forced to try to play the role of integrator across twelve or more different types of agencies and partners.[7]

Even when efforts are executed at the highest level within one or even all of these disciplines, it is a tremendous challenge to coordinate each with what is happening in all of the others to maximize their collective effectiveness and ROI. Unfortunately, this fragmentation and disconnection is occurring at precisely the same moment that uniting these disparate efforts is more critical than ever, as consumers expect more seamless experiences across channels and are moving more frequently and fluidly from one to the other.

So with the opportunities and challenges clear, the question for today's marketer becomes how to most effectively utilize and connect these disparate disciplines to activate behaviors in a best-in-class way, without sacrificing or diluting the power of each. The answers will come in the chapters that follow, and will provide a framework for more effectively managing marketing efforts, departments, and partners, but it will be important to note that the method within begins at the end—with the transaction—and holds at its center the consumer and the unique path each one takes on his or her journey toward it.

We are not alone in the call for marketers to start the planning process at the end of the journey. For instance, Rory Sutherland, vice chairman of Ogilvy Group, in his recommendation, points out that traffic planners of roads and highways use this very approach because it enables them to: "1) start by eliminating isolated bottlenecks before you worry about building a whole new road; and 2) optimise any journey."[8]

Sutherland demonstrates the benefit for marketers with an example: "[I]f your POS is only 50% as good as it could be, then your advertising—however brilliant—will only be working at 50% capacity."[9]

Starting at the end, however, can bring so much more: It can shed light on the multiple, nonlinear paths consumers travel on their shopping journeys; it can provide insights into the key messaging needs and opportunities at each point along them; and it can help to ensure that every point has maximized its ability to contribute to closing the sale before any investment is made in the points prior to deliver more leads to it. Starting at the end is analogous to the process of curriculum development. Educators start with the knowledge and skills students need to have at graduation and then work back toward the starting point to ensure students have the wide range of skills and experience they will need to draw upon along the way.

Once marketers have identified this more powerful starting point—one at the opposite end of the more traditional approach that typically begins with a big, awareness-building idea—the next task is to understand the opportunities and methods to align, unify, and connect all of the disparate marketing disciplines to their greatest, behavior-changing effect.

WELCOME TO THE ACTIVATION IMPERATIVE METHOD

Because activating a brand means activating behaviors in the brand's target consumers, shoppers, or prospects that help move them toward a transaction, the most effective brand activation targets those key moments along the path-to-purchase where there are barriers to overcome or opportunities to accelerate progress toward that ultimate goal.

As a result, the process of activation begins by developing insights into individuals' new, multiple, and increasingly nonlinear paths-to-purchase.

E-commerce, t-commerce (transactions via smart television sets), social media, and mobile technologies have enabled a greater variety of routes by which people can move toward transactions, and the key to activating them is identifying the behavioral inflection points along the way—the points in time where progress tends to stall or accelerate. Using quantitative and qualitative research, as well as database modeling, marketers can identify the critical obstacles or under-leveraged triggers that impact key audiences' movement toward purchase.

In the case of a major manufacturer of health and beauty products struggling to boost sales through a leading big box retailer, the key inflection points turned out to range from pre-trip planning—shoppers did not perceive sufficient savings to warrant waiting to purchase the category on their biweekly stock-up trips at the mass retailer versus during their weekly fill-in trips at grocery—to in-store navigation—shoppers were simply unaware of the health and beauty department's location at the back of the store.

Once these key behavioral points are identified, and the potential to address them is clear, marketers can then deepen their understanding of the interests and motivations of the audience in order to facilitate delivering the kind of value that will engage them at those moments and create the opportunities to inspire behavior change. Depending on the insights gleaned, the range of what individuals value can extend well beyond the merely monetary to include opportunities for self-expression, personalization, experiences, entertainment, access, and even social good.

With that high-level roadmap delineated, several key questions require deeper exploration, namely:

- How does a marketer identify the optimal moments to engage with each consumer, shopper, or prospect, whether to overcome barriers or accelerate movement toward the desired purchase behavior?
- How does a marketer reach consumers/shoppers/prospects at those key moments once they have been identified?
- How does a marketer create sufficient value or incentive for the consumer, shopper, or prospect to engage at those points of contact?
- Once engaged, how does the marketer identify and deliver the right content, message, or offer to the consumer/shopper/prospect to move them closer to purchase?

The answers lie in strategically aligning the numerous, currently fragmented marketing disciplines, from digital, social, and mobile marketing to direct/customer relationship management (CRM), shopper, and experiential to utilize each of their unique capabilities and maximize their total effect.

To achieve that benefit, it is important to highlight the two key foundational principles at the center of the method that follows:

- That the various specialized disciplines must no longer be thought of separately, or even in parallel, but instead as complementary components of an interconnected marketing "ecosystem," in the same way that the neurological, respiratory, and digestive systems are specialized systems with unique requirements and capabilities, but work together synergistically to power a healthy human body.
- That fully embracing each discipline's unique strengths and capabilities can provide a framework for leveraging the key best practices of each more broadly, so as to actually enhance and more effectively reap the benefit of the unique capabilities of the others.

While these ideas and their implications for modern marketing organizations will be fully explained and developed in the coming chapters, it may be helpful to simply consider how a mobile app experience, for example, could benefit from the shopper marketer's expertise in how people utilize technology in the aisles of specific retailers, from the database marketer's expertise in how that shopper can be uniquely identified and presented with content tailored to their interests and experiences, from the participation marketer's tools to better drive interaction and involvement, from the digital marketer's abilities to optimize user experience, and from the mobile marketer's expertise in connecting the right mobile platforms to achieve all of the above.

While mobile not only represents the future of consumer engagement, it also is the simplest way to highlight the need and potential power of unifying currently fragmented disciplines and more broadly unlocking the power of each. Mobile is an inherently one-to-one channel, digitally enabled, socially connected, and utilized across the path-to-purchase to engage with sponsored content and experiences. As a result, it is a helpful shorthand example for the impending requirement and broader opportunity marketers have to fully embrace the unique skills required by each specialized discipline while leveraging their strengths in a broader and more interconnected way.

These ideas will be key to unlocking the full power of any organization's activation efforts. More specifically, as the reader will see in the coming chapters:

- Some of the most sophisticated segmentations of behavior along the path-to-purchase utilized by shopper marketing specialists can leverage mobile and social data to delineate the multiple, nonlinear paths today's consumers/shoppers/prospects follow, and identify key opportunities to impact them.
- New digital and mobile marketing platforms and techniques offer tremendous opportunities to seamlessly interact with individuals in the moments that matter most, as identified by the types of shopper segmentations above.
- Creating engagement with individuals requires creating sufficient value to warrant an interaction, and techniques from participation, experiential, and content marketing can be particularly helpful in achieving it. When those techniques are combined with the abilities to match content with recipients via methods born and bred in the world of direct marketing, the impact can be exponential.
- Determining which branded content, offer, or message to deliver after the initial engagement can leverage the "next best action" approach employed by data scientists versed in the worlds of database marketing and CRM.

The result can be programs powerfully targeted to reach consumers, shoppers, and prospects where there is the greatest opportunity to advance them toward the desired transaction while also delivering a uniquely clear statement about the brand.

A FEW EXAMPLES, PLEASE

As is usually the case, a few focused examples of select activation principles in action can be helpful to understanding the broader opportunity.

Walgreens' battle with CVS to dominate the flu shot market is a particularly illuminating case in point, because in this instance the category is not just commoditized, but the products are in fact, by law, exactly identical. As a result, Walgreens could only achieve its goal of topping its previous year's record of administering one million flu shots by out-activating the competition—which Walgreens did with its "Arm Yourself for the Ones You Love" campaign.[10, 11]

Walgreens' research into consumer shopping behavior in the category identified a segment of "intenders" who had planned to get flu shots, but always reached a point in their paths-to-purchase between intent and transaction, where their families' myriad needs took precedence and they never ultimately purchased a shot for themselves. By understanding that this segment's interests and motivations were caring for others—and in particular, their families—during the busy back-to-school season, the program repositioned its communications to drive engagement by delivering that value; namely, highlighting that getting a flu shot was a way for moms to protect their families by protecting themselves.

To drive this point home in a branded way, anyone who received a flu shot at Walgreens was given a heart-shaped bandage for their arm on which they could write the name of the person they were getting their shot to protect. Moms began to see other moms sporting heart-shaped bandages with their kids' names written on them and sharing the images on Twitter and Facebook, with the effect of each interaction reminding other moms to "arm themselves for the one they love." Concurrently, images of real people striking heroic poses displaying their heart-shaped bandages with loved ones' names began appearing in digital outdoor, print, television, and online, with celebrities like Dr. Oz getting into the act. In just five weeks, Walgreens had delivered more than five million flu shots, exceeding the previous year's record sales by more than 400%.

In another example, a typical key behavioral opportunity for retailers is to increase consumers' time spent in one of their retail environments—be it brick-and-mortar, online, or even printed catalog—as greater time generally results in greater purchase volume.

Ikea's much-awarded program offered consumers the chance to be photographed in a perfect replica of the living room[12] on their catalog's cover and receive a custom-printed catalog featuring that image. It is a great example of an activation program that takes advantage of self-expression, personalization, and unique experiences as sources of value that drive engagement, and does so in a way that reinforces the brand's approachability and user-centeredness. The program impacts behavior in several ways, keeping visitors in proximity of the Ikea store longer (to have their photo taken), and driving an additional visit (to pick up their custom catalog). The program also inevitably encouraged consumers to keep the catalog in their homes longer than usual to show others, thereby creating incremental views and, one can assume, incremental purchases. It also generated additional word of mouth with family and friends, further promoting the brand, the offer, and a store visit.

One of the most effective ways to create future activation is to deliver a uniquely positive consumer experience that memorably conveys a strong sense of the brand and the role it can play in the consumer's life. In fact, activation efforts are particularly powerful in this dual role, because they often drive people to literally experience a brand's product or service, rather than merely defining it.

A great example is Nike+[13], which launched as a program between Nike and Apple to enhance consumers' running experiences by synchronizing music and tracking data during their runs. For years it has built business by adding value to the purchase of both companies' products that differentiated them from the competition at key decision points, driving consumers of one to purchase the other to fully unlock its value, and increasing loyalty for both via furthering integration of each into consumers' daily lives. Simultaneously, it enhanced Nike's brand as the cutting-edge choice for serious runners and Apple's as the leading lifestyle technology brand, leveraging the cross-promotion at its core across PR-generating events, local experiences, training clubs, online, at retail, and via in-app communications.

Properly conceived and executed, these kinds of brand-activation efforts leverage all of the appropriate marketing disciplines in a coordinated way, focused on key behavioral inflection points to motivate actions by consumers that drive a measurable return. It is important to understand, however, that as these examples illustrate, building a brand and building its sales volume not only can go hand in hand—they should.

A LITTLE BRAND-BUILDING HISTORY

To understand the full power of activation, one needs to move beyond the traditional distinctions and separation between brand-building and business-building efforts, and recognize that the most impactful work can do both—and do both more effectively by unlocking the powerful synergies between them.

Traditionally, marketers have looked at their brand- and business-building initiatives as separate efforts with a typically one-way relationship: brand building potentially leading to business building at some future point, but rarely the other way around. Business building was often associated with immediate transaction-driving efforts—such as discounts and couponing—that were thought to effectively drive sales in the near term, but with the perceived cost of eroding a brand's equity over the long term.

Today, there are many who still see these two activities as separate, and, often, believe that one component or the other is not only not needed, but actually detrimental to longer-term efforts.

An example often invoked to demonstrate the paramount power of brand building over business building is Apple. Apple's ever-present marketing is often described as purely brand building, and yet it is perceived as successful at driving business. Even factoring out Apple's product innovation, strategically designed cross-platform ecosystem, and user-centered product design, many fail to notice Apple's characteristically innovative business-building activation programs.

A wonderful case in point is the Apple Genius Bars, which illustrate the power of connecting brand building with business building in one seamless experience. In Apple retail store locations, the Genius Bar offers expert help to potential purchasers in the process of updating or upgrading their hardware. The Genius Bars brilliantly target one of the key obstacles along the path to a technology purchase: the consumer's fear of the time, effort, and inconvenience that will be associated with migrating to new technologies.

The Genius Bar offers a one-stop shop where consumers can get the benefit of a Genius on their side (without being made to feel like an idiot), which literally removes what is often the final barrier to triggering a hardware purchase (inside or outside the store) by assuring consumers that someone will personally and efficiently guide them through the migration process. The Genius, of course, also makes sure that the consumer knows how to take immediate advantage of their new purchase's key features and benefits, creating a positive brand experience from the outset and further reinforcing Apple as the category's most user-friendly brand. The Genius also helps to ensure that the consumer understands how to fully integrate their new technology with the rest of Apple's very sticky ecosystem of products and services, carefully designed to increase loyalty by increasing the inconvenience of any future switching (thereby erecting the same barrier for their competitors that they just overcame).

Apple's other activation programs are also often conveniently over-looked, such as their annual offer of a free iPod or other item[14]—for ex-ample, free Beats Solo2 Headphones in 2015[15] with the purchase of a new laptop—typically timed right before the scheduled launch of a new model. These promotions are generally framed as part of an annual back-to-school special for college students and faculty,[16] and clearly help Apple empty warehouses by offering these price-sensitive back-to-school shoppers an added value and reason to "buy now."

Of course, there are also numerous examples of brands that are very clearly defined and have high awareness, but are still not successfully driving sales—or in some cases, are actually hurting sales. Many may remember the widely popular Taco Bell Chihuahua campaign in 2000, which penetrated the national psyche sufficiently to produce the cultural catchphrase, "Yo Quiero Taco Bell," while sales actually dropped 6%.[17] The long-running Energizer Bunny campaign both created a lot of awareness and helped to sell a lot of batteries—unfortunately, those sales were for Duracell. The campaign is widely associated with actually eroding Energizer sales.[18, 19]

In both cases, the marketers' intent was certainly to build business, but by only focusing on defining the brand and creating awareness for it, they missed opportunities to activate the brand more fully with the right consumers at the right time.

Many of these types of missteps are fueled by antiquated[20] and perhaps overly simplified communication models, such as "AIDA"—in which "A" = attention; "I" = interest; "D" = desire; "A" = action—and the associated linear purchase funnel models that call for shaping attitudes (in AIDA, represented by "desire"), before beginning to shape action (AIDA's final "A").[21, 22, 23]

These models, unfortunately, do not account for the reality of new, mul-tiple, nonlinear paths-to-purchase, or for the fact that by building business, marketers are often able to fund additional marketing activities to further both brand and business. As psychologist and brand strategist Adam Ferrier points out, "This model was developed 100 years ago when advertising was passive—the consumer couldn't be involved. Now there's an interactive mar-keting communications landscape that advertisers can do more than just talk *at* people—they can involve them in the communications."[24]

What's more, these models also overlook several other realities, includ-ing that an action is often the most efficient way to build a brand. As Ferrier

FIGURE 1.1
The old AIDA model.
Source: Designed by Sarah Vonderhaar.

says, "action changes attitude faster than attitude changes actions."[25] In his book, *The Advertising Effect*, he explains that "The reason it works is through psychological principles including cognitive dissonance— we like our thoughts, feelings, and actions to be aligned or we feel uncomfortable. When you involve people in your mission through action, they adapt their thoughts and feelings to make sense of the action."[26] Why action over belief? As Ferrier states, the individual cannot take back the action once it occurs.

On the other side of the all-or-nothing group are online marketers who focus exclusively on driving clicks and conversions, and are explicitly unconcerned with conveying any sense of long-term brand meaning. Many of them argue that branding is losing its power and relevance as shoppers easily access reviews from users and professionals, and compare prices.[27, 28] Powering their argument is the market trend that consumers are indeed becoming less loyal.[29] What their argument overlooks is the emotional component of decision making and the power that brands can play in evoking and connecting to them, as well as the powerful business-building momentum that brands can create by defining experiences and creating meaning that users can remember, speak about, and share.[30]

BETTER BRAND AND BUSINESS BUILDING TOGETHER

The Activation Imperative Method (AIM) is designed to help marketing organizations integrate both long-term brand building and short-term sales building to maximize efficiency and effectiveness in the marketplace.

These principles are as relevant in the consumer marketing realm as they are in business-to-business marketing. While the business-to-business (B2B) path-to-purchase is often longer and includes multiple decision makers, B2B marketers still need to activate behaviors in their audiences to drive sales and maximize marketing ROI. In fact, their smaller, more-defined target audiences and elongated paths-to-purchase can make B2B marketing particularly well suited to enhanced activation efforts.

In the pages that follow we will show how the AIM helps organizations facilitate the alignment of the specialized marketing disciplines and the key roles each discipline plays in achieving the improved results.

We will start by going deeper into the foundational principles of how to best structure brand-building marketing programs across the disciplines so that they will also generate greater sales, loyalty, and ROI. We will discuss how to identify objectives, select strategies, cascade briefs across the disciplines, develop and evaluate creative executions, and manage market implementation—all built on insights into individuals' new, nonlinear paths-to-purchase.

To aid in fully appreciating the challenges, opportunities, and method of this alignment, we will follow by discussing each of the activation disciplines in more detail and analyzing the unique role they can play in the marketing mix, starting with traditional advertising and continuing through shopper, mobile, social, digital, experiential, direct/database marketing, and more. In

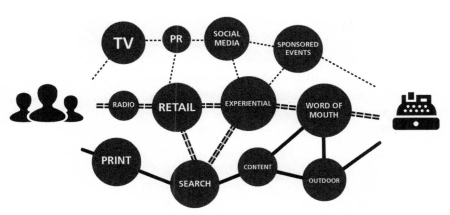

FIGURE 1.2
Consumers now have multiple nonlinear paths-to-purchase.
Source: Designed by Sarah Vonderhaar.

the final chapter, we will provide some guidelines for managing integration, so readers and their organizations can begin to implement the principles immediately and be on their way to more-effective brand activation as quickly and efficiently as possible.

AIM FOR THE TARGET

With the importance of brand activation understood and the ways to achieve it most effectively to be outlined in the pages ahead, it may be helpful at this point to address specifically how organizations should understand and think about the Activation Imperative Method by clarifying precisely what it is and what it is not.

Starting with what it is, it is helpful to consider the entire marketing process as akin to the endeavor of shooting an arrow at a distant target. Of course, when one considers today's marketing planning cycles and the complexity of coordinating its required technologies, channels, and partners, an even more accurate metaphor may be launching a spacecraft to a distant planet.

In either case, the analogy fits because there is an ideal outcome—the arrow striking the center of the bull's-eye, the spacecraft landing at the desired location on a distant planet, or the right message reaching the right prospect at the right time—that is a great distance away in both time and proximity from the initial launch point—the release of the arrow, the launch of the spacecraft, or the beginning of the strategic and creative development process. Even on an abbreviated timeline, most marketers are beginning their planning process months (and in some cases more than a year) before a program will actually be in-market and have the opportunity to reach the target audience in the desired way.

What the arrow (or spacecraft) analogy can help to illustrate is how the tiniest imprecision at the point of launch becomes magnified over time and distance as the arrow (or spacecraft) travels toward its destination. An arrow that is pointed just a fraction of an inch off target at the point of release will be several inches off target once it has traveled ten feet, and several feet off target once it has traveled fifty yards, resulting in not just missing the bull's-eye, but the entire target. In the case of a space launch, a tiny error in initial trajectory can result in hundreds of miles of correction once the spacecraft has reached a distant planet.

The purpose of the AIM is to bring a more methodical and precise approach to the process of aiming at a desired outcome that is a great distance away; in this case, an ideal experience that engages an individual we may never actually see many months in the future. By making sure that we solve the right problems in the right order, we can make incremental improvements in decision making that can have profound effects on the final result, just as that one-tenth-of-an-inch correction in archery can mean the difference between striking the bull's-eye or striking an observer.

If a marketer is able to be even just 1% more effective in who is reached where along their path-to-purchase, 1% more effective in how they are reached, 1% more effective in engaging them at that point of contact, and 1% more effective in the subsequent messages and actions, the compounded effect can be substantial in final results and marketing return. When all of the fragmented marketing disciplines are more effectively coordinated, and each of their best practices more widely leveraged across the others, the increase in effectiveness can, of course, be significantly greater.

Now for what the AIM is not.

The AIM is not an attempt to entice people to buy things that they do not need or want, or to deceive anyone into transactions or engagements that they perceive as anything less than valuable and desirable. The AIM, quite to the contrary, is an attempt to put people at the center of the experience to make sure that as consumers and shoppers they only receive the most relevant information and content at the most appropriate points in their journeys, and that they experience every interaction as so clearly valuable and meaningful that they choose to continue to engage with the brand. The AIM will not and cannot make inferior products or brands seem superior, irrelevant products or brands seem relevant, or products or brands of no value to an individual appear valuable. The AIM is specifically designed to ensure that people's time is valued, by delivering them only the most valuable information at the most relevant places and times; that their desires and interests are valued, by offering the right content to the right person when it is most helpful or desired; and that brands and products of value and relevance are brought to the attention of consumers who will value them as efficiently and effectively as possible.

The AIM is designed to put an end to the useless and irritating "carpet bombing" of messaging that barrages groups of people with unwanted information and sales pitches that are relevant or interesting to but a few. The AIM is designed to bring precision, care, respect, and value to every point of contact so that great brands find their audiences, audiences find their brands, and marketers and consumers find maximum value in every effort.

The key to all of the above is an ethical, high-integrity approach to the business of marketing, but it is also the growing capability to utilize data to create value for individuals and brands.

The information and insights about individual behaviors now available to savvy marketers have the power to be either a blunt instrument used to try to pound target audiences into submission based on inside information regarding their supposed needs and wants, or a welcome level of understanding that can be used to effectively and respectfully separate the messaging wheat from the chaff on an individual level, to the benefit of consumers everywhere. The former will never work long-term, falling into the old-school trap of trying to drive short-term business results to the detriment of long-term brand building, while the latter is the only way to create truly sustainable value for consumers and marketers, by optimally building business and brand to the mutual benefit of both.

Interestingly, the technologies that have made possible the increase in information and insight available to marketers have also increased the information and insight available to consumers regarding the brands that surround them. The result is an unprecedented level of transparency that quickly exposes brands whose behaviors do not match their promises, ensuring that even those not motivated by integrity or authenticity will soon be motivated by business reality.

For all of the challenges and opportunities that the new influx and accessibility of data have created, and which will need to be meaningfully addressed by marketers, individuals, and society as a whole, one thing is clear: Brands that behave inauthentically, inconsistently, or shortsightedly will quickly be identified as such, reducing any perceived near-term business benefits and increasing long-term brand erosion. That reality will certainly be to the benefit of authentic brands, and the consumers who love them, everywhere.

A WORD ABOUT WORDS

It is worthy of note that discussing marketing can often feel like working at the Tower of Babel. Within even a single company, a key marketing term can be used in different ways in different departments or on different floors. Marketing terms evolve and meanings change at a dizzying rate. For example, to some a "brand" can mean a logo and its color palette, while for others it means the implied promise of how people will benefit from using its products. For a third group, it could mean the product itself.

In the following pages, we will do our best to define terms as we go to preserve clarity. When we are discussing an alternative meaning of the word, we will acknowledge the difference. While there are always those who will espouse points of view that "Everything is brand building/business building/retail/social/etc."—and they will certainly have a point—we will endeavor to use definitions in the most broadly understood and hopefully productive ways, and ask our readers to try to understand our intent, so the discussion can focus on the ideas versus the nomenclature. We will attempt to elevate the discussion beyond semantics to help marketers meaningfully address their daily realities. The marketing world is at a unique point where the powers driving fragmentation are now beginning to drive convergence. The resulting overlap of ideas, disciplines, and efforts can certainly be confusing, but the opportunities for improvement are tremendous.

As many have no doubt observed, when one speaks with a practitioner of any one of the major marketing disciplines, the practitioner will often explain that their respective discipline is the key to all effective marketing efforts. As we will discover in the chapters ahead, they are all right—at least to some extent—as we delineate how to apply each discipline's perspective and practices to the greatest effect.

Just think: A damaging economic downturn coupled with the disruptive chaos and empowerment of technological innovation might have set the marketing world on a path to more-effective brand and business building. Read on, and see for yourself.

2

Ready, Set, AIM

Brand activation can be viewed as both an outcome and a process. From either perspective, however, it requires inspiring real behaviors by real people.

As challenging as behavior change can be to accomplish, particularly in an increasingly fast-paced and distracted world, full of conflicting desires, obligations, and agendas, it is an objective that offers the marketer one notable advantage: it is inherently measurable.

Where there is behavior, there is action, and where there is action, there is evidence of that action that can be observed, recorded, and quantified. As a result, marketers are not forced to identify proxies for attitudes, intent, or other qualitative indicators of interest and affection that are assumed to one day in the future lead to transactions. They can instead know when an activation effort bears fruit, and how much. They can also know when a subsequent effort bears more fruit more efficiently.

Creating that kind of measurable improvement is the purpose and focus of the Activation Imperative Method.

BEGIN WITH A BASELINE

To quantify improvement, the activation process needs to begin from the point that there are baseline measurements in place that capture an organization's key performance indicators (KPIs) and represent its current marketing practices applied with their typical effectiveness. From unit sales to store visits to average basket size, the organization's marketing function needs to be measuring what is important and, therefore, have a general sense of expected results associated with expected efforts under expected market conditions.

These measurements are the foundation from which improvement in activation efforts can be made and measured. If these measures are not in place, there will not only be no way to identify incremental increases in effectiveness and efficiency, but there will also be no way to begin the process of identifying the key behaviors that impact the marketers' uniquely selected KPIs.

To be clear, there is no single, one-size-fits-all solution that will be effective or even appropriate for the wide range of potential marketing challenges organizations may face. Every business situation is unique, and must be appreciated as such, from the nuances of the product category, competitive set, target consumer, and path-to-purchase to the industry dynamics, market dynamics, consumer life cycle, and cultural context.

But while there may not be one single solution, there are in fact principles and approaches that can be applied to any and every marketing challenge, even if ultimately when applied they lead the marketer to an appropriately unique course of action.

These principles are helpful precisely because of the fact that they transcend the specifics of any given situation and have relevance and impact across the emergence of new technology platforms, media channels, or trends. The approaches move beyond simple best practices to offer a practical methodology to address marketing challenges that helps to ensure that marketers and their organizations approach each opportunity in the most systematic, disciplined, and rigorous ways possible to guarantee maximum effectiveness and efficiency. Marketers will then not only be inoculated against simply chasing the latest "me too" trend of the day, but will also know precisely if they should—and if so, how to—apply all the key marketing disciplines in combination in order to achieve the greatest advantage in their own unique situation.

ALIGNING THE KEY PERFORMANCE INDICATORS

The AIM begins with organizational—or at least marketing leadership's—alignment on the selected KPIs, as well as a sense of the current baseline performance around each. This is much more than an academic exercise. This is the critical step of an organization's leadership aligning on what will be measured, and therefore, how the organization will track its own progress and define its success. These KPIs are also the foundation for all of the work to come, as the embodiment and quantification of the behavioral outcomes we aspire to optimize with brand activation through the AIM.

To use a concrete example, if a quick service restaurant (QSR) identifies same store sales versus the same period the previous year as a KPI, they may also choose to measure daily visits and average check size by store as additional KPIs to enable them to better understand the drivers of same store sales and track their progress in creating the basis to improve them. The organization has now not only clarified how it defines and measures success, but it can also begin with the end in mind by moving backwards up the path-to-purchase to identify the key behaviors behind what is being measured.

This is one of the foundational approaches to brand activation, and the AIM in particular. The more precisely the desired business results have been identified, the more precisely the associated behaviors can be identified as well.

In the case of the aforementioned quick service restaurant, the key behaviors of how frequently one chooses to visit (versus visiting a competitor's restaurant or not eating out at all) and how much one chooses to order at that visit can be identified as the next most proximate behaviors to the business results. From there, the process can continue to identify the behaviors that impact those behaviors, and therefore determine where the behavioral "off-ramps" (points shoppers may depart the path prior to transaction) and "on-ramps" (points shoppers may join the path toward transaction) may lie, so that the marketer can more effectively facilitate the ultimately desired behaviors. In the QSR example, the key behavior of choosing to visit (or not) the brand's restaurant may be impacted by the behavior of extending a lunch invitation instead of dining alone, or the behavior of driving to lunch versus walking.

What these examples illustrate is that while all of the marketing disciplines have the potential to activate, when the key behaviors have been identified, it becomes easier to determine which disciplines can most effectively and efficiently seize the behavioral opportunity, how, and in which combination. In the case of our quick service restaurant, one can imagine a social media initiative that encourages new and existing "lunch buddies" to share their unique stories in exchange for two-for-one deals. Or the approach may be a socially driven healthy lifestyle program introducing the "walking lunch" as an alternative to the all-too-common working lunch, with offers linked to a phone's pedometer app that leverage the restaurant's advantage in proximity.

In these two examples, the optimal solution may turn out to be a social media program tied to a retail promotion enabled via mobile that feeds into a database loyalty program for ongoing one-to-one rewards and incentives. Whatever the outcome, this simply illustrates how following key behaviors backwards from the ultimate KPIs can lead to the identification of preceding behaviors that disciplines can be aligned to impact.

THE NEXT BEHAVIORAL CHALLENGE

Once the behavioral opportunities have been delineated and the disciplines best suited to addressing them identified, the next challenge becomes determining how to utilize the selected disciplines to impact the desired behaviors in a way that both creates sufficient value for the consumer/shopper/prospect to engage and uniquely expresses key attributes of the brand.

Starting with the second goal first, the objective is to create a program that so clearly and uniquely embodies the brand that even without a logo, audiences would know that it was an effort from the brand and not one of its competitors.

In addition to simply utilizing the brand's tone of voice and look-and-feel, the actual type of tactic or program can be conceived and executed in a way that is not just consistent with the brand, but an embodiment of it. The goal is that the consumer, shopper, or prospect is not merely reached at the right point along their path-to-purchase and engaged to change behavior, but that the encounter becomes a true brand experience, defining its meaning as well as reinforcing its attributes and appeal to the individual.

A great example of a strongly branded activation program is the Coca-Cola "Share a Coke" campaign. Built on their brand attributes of spreading happiness, people could find their names—or those of their friends and family—on bottles of Coke and Diet Coke. People could create their own virtual bottles on a special website and share them via social media or shareacoke.com. They could also create unique Coke bottles to order or find the most popular names at stores. At selected events, they were able to personalize two mini Coke cans—one to keep and one to share[1]—and on shareacoke.com, they could look up facts about their name, driving further brand engagement by offering information about something people truly care about—themselves.[2] Of course, they could also earn points for sharing with My Coke Rewards.

Just recall the classic commercial "I'd Like to Buy the World a Coke" and one can see, in the words of that commercial's cocreator, the embodiment of the brand "as a social catalyst,"[3] which is clearly brought to life in the Share a Coke activation program.

Meanwhile, Pepsi has long positioned itself as being the choice of today.[4] One of their classic taglines, "Choice of the New Generation,"[5] evolved from "The Pepsi Generation," and after losing their way for a bit during their Pepsi Refresh program, they recently brought the idea to life with the campaign tagline, "Live for Now."[6] When they ran the Refresh program, Pepsi lost substantial market share to their rival, dropping to third behind Coke and Diet Coke.[7] To explore the drop, Pepsi conducted extensive "focus groups, in-house ethnographies, quantitative and qualitative studies and cultural immersions"[8] throughout the world.

Their findings about how people differentiated between Coke and Pepsi were not surprising, namely: "Coke is timeless. Pepsi is timely." Summarizing the findings to *Advertising Age*, Pepsi's then president—global enjoyment and chief creative officer, Brad Jakeman—reportedly said, "Understanding our famous past is important in rewriting a more famous future."[9]

To bring this promise to life, Pepsi has tended to run programs that take swipes at their main competitor by positioning it as out of step with consumers' modern tastes, from the Pepsi Challenge in 1981, which invited consumers to compare the two brands in a blind taste test, to a program in 2015 that gave away tickets based around the theme, "But Only with Pepsi,"[10] which invited consumers to visit the Pepsi Pass website for the chance to win admission to the season's hottest events.

As these examples demonstrate, these competitors' very different brand foundations lead them to very different tactical solutions to achieve engagement. Both solutions, however, clearly embody their respective brand promises and advance their brands' equities (though we suspect one is advancing more than the other).

The other half of the engagement challenge for the marketer is creating sufficient value to drive participation by the consumer, shopper, or prospect. Before that discussion can begin, it is critical to understand that in many cases the consumer and the shopper may not be the same individual.

In our quick service restaurant example, it is likely that the ultimate consumer of the dining experience was the person shopping for it. But imagine that the shopper was a working mom (or dad) looking to bring home dinner for her children before she attends a work event. In this case, it is not the consumer of the brand's products (the children) who are making the purchase decision—it is the shopper (the mom or dad). This situation is frequently the case in packaged-goods marketing, where the shopper is often a parent choosing grocery items, such as soft drinks or snacks, for the ultimate consumers at home. It can also be the case in B2B scenarios where an individual or department makes the purchase decision for a different set of end users within an organization.

THE SHOPPER AND THE CONSUMER

It is important in brand activation, and a key aspect of the AIM, to not only clearly identify both the shopper and the consumer when they are different individuals, but also to understand their interrelationship behaviorally along the path-to-purchase.

In most cases, our focus will be on the shopper—the person making the ultimate purchase decision—but the needs, wants, and behaviors of the consumer will often be very important to the shopper, and therefore relevant and important to understand. While Mom may be making the decisions about which snack to buy for her children, she may be open to trying new options that could make her a hero with her children, perhaps by selecting a brand that offers a coveted premium from the summer's hottest movie, or even a chance to win VIP tickets to the "big game." In those cases, the consumer may not only be the ultimate end user of the product, but also a critical influencer whose interests and, therefore, behaviors become another key touchpoint along the shopper's path-to-purchase.

This dynamic, and the previously discussed behaviors, are why the AIM begins with a deep understanding of the shopper (versus simply the consumer) and his or her unique path-to-purchase. The deepest and most robust insights into the dynamics and influences on shoppers along their journeys, both inside and outside of retail environments, currently reside with the industry's leading shopper marketers.

A common misconception regarding shopper marketing is that it is exclusively focused on messaging and offers within a brick-and-mortar retail environment. Of course, in today's technology-enabled world, every environment is a retail environment, and the best shopper marketers have always studied the entire shopper journey and leveraged a variety of tools to reach shoppers at all of the critical points along the way, whether it culminates in-store or online.

This approach has become particularly fruitful in recent years as mobile, social, and other digital platforms have enabled a new set of nonlinear paths-to-purchase. Gone are the days when there was but one single, sequential path that the vast majority of shoppers traveled. Now a shopper may choose to research his or her purchase prior to visiting a retail store via a whole new variety of channels, choose to do their research via a mobile app standing in the aisle, or choose to simply seek recommendations from friends via social media and then buy online.

Even the same media channels can be used in multiple ways, with one shopper using social media to brag about a purchase after it has been made and another using it to research one prior. The emergence of these new channels and new technologies has now created multiple nonlinear paths-to-purchase, shifting sophisticated marketers' various approaches from exclusively focusing on consumer segmentations to actually beginning to develop shopper segmentations. This can be critical to effective marketing, not only because there are now myriad ways to consider and make purchases, but also because of the differences in how a single individual may shop different product categories or behave in different types of retailer environments, all of which present tremendous opportunities for the marketer to activate behavior.

SAME SHOPPER, SAME CATEGORY, DIFFERENT CHANNEL

One of the clearest examples to illustrate the point might be the contrast in behaviors that the same shopper will exhibit shopping the same category in two different retail channels: convenience stores versus club stores. A single man stopping into a convenience store for a soft drink is generally in a mission-based shopping mode, stopping for a chilled single-serve size for immediate consumption alone, or for a chilled six-pack or two-liter bottle for consumption with others at an upcoming destination. This will be a mission-based visit with a clear and specific objective and the desire to get in and out quickly, as the shopper is likely in transit to another destination. As a result, there will be little treasure hunting by the shopper once inside the store. Instead, there will more often than not be a beeline for the cooler followed by a beeline to the register, and back to the car.

When that same single man shops at his local club store he is most likely in a stock-up mode, thinking about the many future usage occasions that he is looking to address with this one visit, and the club store is his destination, with adequate time allotted for it. He is therefore more likely to be open to new discoveries as he traverses many more aisles of his club store than he ever would have at his convenience store. Because his shopping behavior is different, the opportunities to influence his behavior are different and must be accounted for.

As a result, the soft drink marketer, in this case, cannot think about a single path-to-purchase, but must instead consider a variety of purchase paths not only taken by different individuals, but in this case, even by the same individual depending on the retail channel.

POWERFUL POINTS ON A PATH-TO-PURCHASE

As one backs out from the actual point of transaction, it is easy to see why the opportunities closest to it can be the most powerful. In the case of packaged-goods marketers—who do not control and in most cases do not even possess their own retail environments—the first marketing challenge can be with the retailer. To even be able to create the presence, messaging, or incentives the marketer needs in the retail environment requires the buy-in and collaboration of the retailer. This challenge of winning with the retailer in order to be able to win with the shopper has also traditionally been the purview of the shopper marketer, who knows how to construct programs that not only appeal to shoppers, but also to the retailer who is the gatekeeper of the store or e-commerce environment.

All of this serves to further highlight the importance of beginning with a comprehensive and insightful analysis of the shoppers' paths-to-purchase and, depending on the variability, potentially a shopper segmentation. These insights will not only uncover the multiple paths shoppers take and the key inflection points along each route, but will also identify opportunities for the brand to collaborate with key retail partners to help them win with their shoppers by utilizing the communications channels they control to do so. Helping the retailer win helps the brand win, and it can be the difference between outselling a key competitor in that channel or being outsold by them.

This type of shopper journey research can be conducted in a myriad of ways, from the old-fashioned shop-along, where a researcher follows shoppers through the experience, taking notes and asking questions; to utilizing a mobile ethnography tool, where shoppers employ their mobile phones to capture their own shopping journey, complete with time and location data and their own qualitative editorial at key milestones; to social listening and pixel tracking. Regardless of the method, this foundational learning is key to brand activation and to the AIM. Properly done, it can identify key barriers and opportunities along the path-to-purchase, and possibly even uncover new potential targets, as current off-ramps are identified along with the shoppers who are currently taking them.

This is yet another important reason to begin at the end by understanding who is currently buying and how their journey unfolded from the transaction back. New opportunity targets (and therefore sources of volume) can emerge that have much in common with current consumers, and could in fact join them should a late-stage exit path be addressed. This is also our first example of how to unlock the full power of one of the currently fragmented marketing disciplines, in this case, shopper marketing, by utilizing its unique strength in uncovering insights into shoppers' true paths-to-purchase, identifying the corresponding shopper segments, and delineating the key touchpoints along each shopper's path. By utilizing shopper marketing expertise in this way, the marketer has the first piece in place to begin to align the roles of the other disciplines around how the brand's consumers shop and buy, as well as to align the roles of the disparate retail channels and partners, and develop programs to leverage the retailer-controlled touchpoints to their greatest potential and impact.

Once that foundational construct is developed, the result will be a shopper-based alignment of media channels both inside and outside of retail environments, targeting key behaviors that can make the difference between a realized transaction and a near miss. It is easy to see how at this point a series of strategic and creative briefs can cascade from this foundation. For example, when a marketer realizes that their brand's potential consumers are researching features and benefits via social media, and that this is a key inflection point where the path-to-purchase either accelerates or deviates, one can imagine briefing a social media team to develop ideas on how to implement programs or incentives that ensure the brand's currently happy consumers are sharing their positive experiences with the brand more actively within their social graphs and spotlighting key messages that have been identified to be particularly important to future shoppers.

The same kind of approach can be utilized with briefs focused on leveraging the key points in each relevant retail environment, from creating experiential programs at the right time and place along the shopper's journey, to more impactfully organizing content on a website.

THE VALUE OF ENGAGEMENT
The key question in each of these briefs, however, will center on how to create sufficient interest and engagement on the part of the shopper, which, as always, will require creating sufficient value from the shopper's perspective to warrant attention, and ultimately participation. This is where the expertise and best practices from participation marketing can be brought to bear, all of which center around the many ways brands can create value for their consumers, shoppers, and prospects.

What individuals value can extend beyond the simply financial, such as discounts, to include unique opportunities for experiences, entertainment, connection, social good, self-expression, and more. Utilizing any or all sources of potential value in ways unique to the brand and appropriate for the audience can increase the likelihood of engagement and ultimately participation. This can often be where borrowed interest, sponsorships, or partnerships can be helpful. When a shopper has limited interest in or awareness of a brand, leveraging a relevant passion point such as music, sports, or fashion with an exclusive opportunity for high-value content or access, for example, when properly done can not only create engagement with the brand and association with key attributes, but also communicate the essence, key features, benefits, or other important aspects of the brand.

One passion area for many is protecting the environment. So building on their equity in their polar bear icon and advancing a relationship they had in place since 2007, Coca-Cola teamed with the World Wildlife Fund in 2011 to create a worthy-cause program called Arctic Home. Aimed at protecting wild polar bears and their habitats through research and the creation of a conservation plan, Arctic Home raised more than $3 million in the first two years of the program, and then expanded from North America to include seventeen European countries as well.[11] In 2012, Coca-Cola announced a continuation of their relationship with the World Wildlife Fund until at least 2020.[12]

Polar bears first appeared in a print ad for Coca-Cola in 1922, and the brand icons expanded into television in 1993 in a commercial entitled

"Northern Lights."[13] So the Arctic Home program and its use of polar bears fit within the brand's iconography were consistent with its mission "to inspire moments of optimism and happiness," and were true to its brand values, including leadership ("The courage to shape a better future") and account-ability ("If it is to be, it's up to me").[14] Perhaps most importantly, however, the program also supported and enabled its consumers' interest in advancing social good, and therefore created value for them and engagement that went beyond their enjoyment of a soft drink.

Once opportunities like this—those that create value and engagement in a way that is consistent with the brand—are identified and aligned with the key behavioral inflection point, the next challenge is how to deliver the right offer to the right individual at the right time. This is where digital channels, and mobile in particular, offer tremendous opportunities to reach shoppers along their journey, and database marketing can guide to whom what offer is made, depending on what is known about the shopper at each respective point of contact. The uniquely tailored response made by the marketer may simply be to align a shopper with the right retailer based on proximity or basic demo-graphic information; or it can be as sophisticated as predictively modeled fi-nancial incentives weighted to the individual's immediate or long-term value to the brand. In either case, at this point in the process, digital and mobile can be employed as the communication channels capable of reaching the shopper at the right time and place to deliver targeted messaging and incentives that maximize effectiveness based on what is known about the shopper.

One of the many reasons attribution (i.e., the ability to accurately correlate a marketing touchpoint with a resulting transaction) has become such a hot topic of conversation in the industry is that the increasing complexity of pur-chase paths and the multiplicity of devices delivering content are requiring new technology solutions to determine which touchpoints deserve credit for impacting any given transaction. Companies that transact online and those without sales through channel partners are way ahead in this regard, given their clearer lines of sight, but the rest of the industry is quickly catching up. Most marketers have moved well beyond the last touch attribution methods of the past, where disproportionate credit is given to the touchpoint closest to transaction, and many are utilizing complex models to isolate media chan-nel effects. Clearly, as omni-channel marketing evolves to include more and more marketers with a unified single view of their consumers across channels and devices, the precision with which marketing messages and delivery can be optimized will only increase, enabling all of the approaches above to be applied in a truly one-to-one way.

A NEW BRIEFING METHOD

One can imagine the strategic and creative briefs cascading from the shopper journey, to how to best create value and participation, to how to deliver the offer at the right time, to how to deliver the right offer to the right shopper. Each team is briefed not only based on the target shopper and key brand attributes, but also on the insights of the previous strategic and creative direction, with each team's outputs evaluated against the same.

One can also imagine how this interconnected approach to the marketing disciplines can lead to a marketing ecosystem, where each discipline plays its role but leverages its strengths across all. Consider, for a moment, the power of each discipline fully realized.

From shopper marketing, every communication is based on deep insight into the shopper's unique path-to-purchase and the behavioral barriers that can stop it or opportunities that can accelerate it. Every in-market activity is aligned with the most appropriate retail channel or partner, and is designed to take full advantage of all that channel or those partners can offer.

From participation marketing, every invitation to participate is experienced as extremely relevant and highly valuable to the shopper, creating an experience that not only is unique to the brand, but also communicates the brand's key features and benefits while incenting behaviors that move the shopper closer to a transaction.

From digital and mobile marketing, there is an always-on ability to have these uniquely valuable brand interactions in a way that is designed around the user and responsive to the device through which it is being experienced. Each leverages all of the most appropriate functionality of the device's technologies to deliver the most value with the least friction, effortlessly providing and receiving information in real time.

From CRM/database marketing, only the offers and content that are most relevant to the individual are delivered, creating mass micro-personalization that makes every interaction with the brand truly tailored to the individual, their likes and dislikes, past purchases, and current needs. Additionally, the process of optimizing those communications would be ongoing, with each new interaction teaching the marketer how to best communicate with the individual and potentially others like him or her.

From experiential and content marketing, people with no previous connection to the brand would be engaged with compelling information or experiences of such value that they would happily opt in to receive future communications, creating the foundation for personalized content going forward.

These happy consumers would then be incented to share their amazing experiences and love of the brand on social media, providing potential future consumers with the testimonials they may need when researching or the validation they may crave post-purchase.

It may all seem like a bridge too far, but the technology and ability to utilize it are here now. Why more marketers are not is a complex question, but is no doubt largely due to the organizational silos that have developed around the fragmented marketing landscape and inhibit synergies. An organization's CRM leader likely has external CRM partners and a CRM budget, and connecting those efforts with the shopper marketing leader/partners/budget takes courage and the willingness to share success.

The other inhibitor is that those stakeholders may be unnecessarily pigeonholed. The CRM group may simply be considered the keepers of the brand's loyalty program, instead of the group trying to leverage individual shopper insights and always identifying the next best action. The shopper marketing group may be simply considered the managers of the retail tasks and relationships, instead of experts in how people buy, as well as the opportunities tied to each retail channel. The mobile team may be focused on an app, rather than ensuring that all of the disciplines above reside in a best-in-class way on the phones in their consumers' pockets.

The goal of the AIM is to help provide marketing organizations with a methodical approach to aligning and managing these disparate disciplines and departments that calibrates each decision point more effectively to ultimately drive the greatest behavioral impact and ROI in the marketplace. Because as marketers everywhere shift their focus from simply brand building to true business building, by fully activating their brands, they will quickly confront the fragmentation and separation still far too ingrained in the current specialist ecosystem. They may gamely try to encourage collaboration and cooperation, even aligning all parties around a single "big idea" via an interagency team, but without the methodology for integration and the ability to leverage each discipline in the most broadly effective and synergistic way, the result may be little more than the uniformity of matching luggage.

If, however, the disciplines align around the key shopper behaviors that most impact the end-goal KPIs, and work backward from there, leveraging each discipline's unique strengths to enhance the others, the collaboration will be more constructively focused and the opportunities for measurable improvements in results more fully realized. There will always be a need, of course, to create that initial interest and awareness, so we will discuss the evolving role of traditional media advertising in our next chapter.

FIGURE 2.1
Building on their equity in their polar bear icon, Coca-Cola teamed with the World Wildlife Fund to create a worthy-cause program.
Source: Glyn Lowe / CC BY-ND 2.0.

3

Broadcast, Billboards, Branding, and More

Television, radio, print; media and industry pundits have long been predicting their demise, and, along with it, the advertising that has supported them. Many have claimed that as media they are simply no longer effective. These types of prophecies are evident in titles and content from the academic and trade press to the popular. To get a sample, simply search terms such as "end of advertising," "end of branding," "branding is dead," or anything similar. You will find one overriding prediction: So-called traditional media channels such as television, radio, and print would die as the world transitioned to online and social media. After all, so the arguments go, there are only so many hours in a day—and audiences will continue to fragment.

Summing up the situation, ad luminary Alex Bogusky said in a conversation with one of us, "I don't know why there's such self-loathing in the industry, but ever since I've been in advertising, practitioners have been predicting its demise."[1]

Of course, the pundits were partly correct in that pure brand awareness, mass media advertising is no longer at the center of the marketing world. But they failed to realize that media consumption, as Artie Bulgrin, senior vice president of Global Research + Analytics at ESPN, points out, is "not a zero sum game." Online and social channels did not replace what was once called "traditional media." They added to it.[2]

The reality is that people are consuming more media than ever—often at the same time—although the delivery methods have clearly changed. Average media consumption has increased from 646 minutes a day in 2010 to 724 minutes a day in 2015.[3] Television is now watched on phones and computers, and includes streaming services; radio is broadcast over the Internet; and magazines and newspapers are distributed via mobile apps. No news here, except that the sky did not fall as predicted—and all forms of media are still supported by brand advertising.

The doom-saying pundits failed to realize that social, public relations (PR), and word of mouth, while immensely powerful, do not operate in a vacuum, and are not always the most effective or efficient ways for people to initially learn about a product, service, or the meaning of a brand. The pundits ignored the possibility that cumulatively encountering a brand across multiple, strategically selected media channels could be more effective, that videos and other shared media rarely become viral on their own and are more often kick-started with paid media seeding,[4] and that pure search marketing might not be sufficient to establish a brand and communicate its proposition.

Rather, people may need to become aware of and interested in a brand before social or PR or even search can give them sufficient reason to visit the brand's website to find out more. In short, it is the overall marketing program that makes the difference, and that program can often effectively leverage so-called traditional media to activate the brand and its prospects.

Unfortunately, many continue to mistakenly view brand activation as somehow in opposition to traditional media channels. Whether this is because brand activation efforts often effectively leverage nontraditional channels, because the industry's increased focus on activation coincided with the rise of new digital media platforms, or because shifting the conversation beyond merely generating awareness is somehow interpreted as a lack of interest in mass media vehicles in general, positioning activation in contrast to traditional media is an inaccurate and misguided perspective.

Additionally, many see digital as being a more cost-effective marketing platform, without calculating the higher labor costs often associated with it.

Every marketer needs to methodically identify the right formula for their brands based on their unique consumer, shopper, and category dynamics, and should never accept nor discount any approach out of hand simply because others are. Inevitably, however, when a brand appears to be built solely by PR, social, word of mouth, or some other discipline or tactic, there are those who will claim that everyone should follow that lead. But bandwagon approaches are a sure way to end up as marketing wallpaper, with competitors and others suddenly all executing the same playbook at the same time in a bid to get noticed. In reality, those moments may turn out to be precisely the right time to embrace an approach others are ignoring.

It is this type of bandwagon thinking, however, coupled with an ever-changing media landscape, that has led some marketers to question their use of television, radio, and print.[5] Nevertheless, traditional brand communication vehicles such as broadcast (including pre-roll), radio (including terrestrial and online), and print advertising can still play a vital role in the new world of brand activation when they are strategically deployed to help facilitate behavior change. In some instances, that can simply be by fulfilling their long-standing missions of generating awareness, interest, and desire that ultimately facilitates inspiring action within the context of broader activation programs. Just take a look at the hugely successful Snickers "You're Not You When You're Hungry" campaign, which launched via broadcast television during the Super Bowl in 2010.[6] The campaign continued to drive talk value via a substantial PR effort focused on the use of Betty White, and was extended with print, social, and increased merchandising levels at retail to activate transactions at the point of purchase.

Prior to the launch, Snickers was a declining brand.[7] But the campaign effort was able to help reverse the trend, reestablishing the brand's place in popular culture with a new take on its hunger-satisfying benefit, and as a result, growing sales volume in the United States by 8% within its first three months. The campaign was successful globally as well. By 2014, Snickers became the world's top-selling candy bar.[8] The broadcast and print advertising portion of the campaign proved to be a powerful and efficient tool for conveying the revamped Snickers brand story, evolving the brand image and enhancing its perceived value, so that at the point of transaction its hunger-busting messaging, limited-edition bars, and activations around new sizes and packs could more effectively drive sales.

Traditional paid media can also be the spark that gets viewers talking via social media or drives them to learn more online, which is why so many Internet-based brands—from Google, Amazon, Facebook, and Kayak to Travelocity, LegalZoom, ancestry.com, and others—choose to advertise on broadcast television.

So how should a marketer best determine if traditional media advertising should be employed in their brand-activation efforts, and when? The answer depends on the target consumer/shopper's path-to-purchase. In fact, understanding that path will not only help determine if and when traditional brand communications are needed, but it will also help to identify their specific roles in how the campaign will help move consumers toward a transaction. In turn, it can also help to determine the style and content of that messaging.

FROM AWARENESS TO ACTION TO ANSWERS

A simple way to think about the role of traditional media advertising as a tool for the AIM is to look at the behavioral and belief needs of the target segments before, during, and after transactions.

While it is widely understood that broadcast television spots (or online pre-roll video), as well as radio (both terrestrial and online) and print advertising, can be very effective in creating brand awareness and demonstrating a product's features and benefits, they can also be utilized to provide the social proof that makes a brand seem legitimate and specific purchasing behaviors more acceptable. This approach was utilized very effectively in a 2011 campaign for Trojan condoms designed to remove the stigma of women selecting and purchasing the product. In this campaign, the advertising departed from the category's traditional male-dominated imagery to depict couples in a pharmacy, where it was the female who was front and center as the one who purchased the product.[9]

The social proof created by traditional media advertising can also impact retailers as much as consumers, creating the impression of market activity and broad-based interest that can encourage retailers to stock more products and/or choose to participate in a manufacturer-driven activation program. Communicating to retailers the size of the media support behind a brand is often sufficient, but actually seeing the campaign as a consumer would can increase the impact on the retailer. In either case, the result can be more opportunities for the marketer to engage consumers and change behavior in and around the retailer's points of purchase.

Another compelling advantage that can come with this type of traditional advertising is the chance for the manufacturer to offer to a select retailer tagging opportunities at the end of broadcast spots or on print and radio ads in exchange for stocking more product and/or featuring them more prominently. It is an old-school tactic that is often overlooked, but it can be an effective strategy to get more presence in key retail channels, which in itself can be enough to activate incremental transactions.

As part of a comprehensive activation program, traditional advertising vehicles can also be used to broadly communicate participation opportunities and other calls to action, including inviting prospects to enter contests, informing them of time-sensitive offers, encouraging them to share their product stories and experiences via social media, or incenting them to engage with the brand in other ways. In our multiscreen world, where more and more frequently consumers are experiencing content on television, for example, while utilizing a mobile device to browse online, television and radio can potentially even inspire prospects to make an immediate purchase.

There is, however, another benefit of traditional advertising that is rarely talked about but can be very powerful in driving activation: its impact on the brand's or its retailer's employee behavior.

Employees can be a walking representation of a brand and can serve as a key influencer during pivotal inflection points along the path-to-purchase. For brands that inhabit multiple retailers, e-commerce sites, markets, or even countries, traditional media advertising can help internal stakeholders and others in the channel to understand the brand's essence, higher purpose, and personality—and even demonstrate expected behaviors by its consumers or shoppers. This can help associates and other internal influencers to more effectively impact the consumers and shoppers with whom they interact.

Some marketers, particularly for service brands, have successfully employed media advertising to achieve these types of goals. "We got the client to do a brand campaign that said they were more than a card," said Steve Hayden, then vice chairman of Ogilvy & Mather, to one of us in an interview about a campaign he helped create for American Express. "We took all of the components of the American Express brand and put them together in corporate messaging that reminded the employees, first of all, of the important global scale and quality of the company."[10]

In other words, knowing that employees would pay special attention to its broadcast advertising, a global media campaign helped the brand enhance morale and bring internal alignment around the key brand attributes they needed to convey no matter where their office was located.

Another potentially powerful role for traditional advertising vehicles can be at the end of the path-to-purchase. Following a transaction, particularly those with numerous choices,[11] some consumers may experience buyer's remorse, leading them to question or second-guess their selection post-purchase. This well-known emotion, unfortunately for the marketer, occurs precisely when other potential buyers would likely be asking the individual about their recent purchase, and when the marketer would prefer the purchaser to be sharing their delight with the product and brand in glowing terms on social media.

Since purchasers are "inclined to pay more attention to advertising of the brand they have purchased,"[12] it can play a critical role in helping to reassure them that they have made a good decision, addressing possible remorse with reminders of benefits and value,[13] as well as providing language on how to think and talk about the brand they bought. It should be noted, however, that when purchasers have negative experiences with a brand or product, positive advertising messages can actually decrease their satisfaction,[14] so this strategy might not work in all instances.

To help rethink and more fully understand how to get the most out of traditional advertising in brand-activation efforts, let's consider the roles of the various forms of traditional advertising—television, radio, print, and out of home—and how each will evolve as the power of addressable media becomes fully realized. We will start with television and then explore radio, print, and out of home, before concluding the chapter with some thoughts on how to best brief teams and partners so they can most effectively create traditional media messaging that builds brand while building business.

HOW SHOULD ONE BE ADDRESSED?

Ad legend Roy Grace said about the power of television advertising, "Television is theater. It's entertainment. Because of that, I just think it carries more weight, more excitement, and more sex appeal."[15] Fortunately, that sex appeal, as we have outlined above, can be very effectively put to work to activate behaviors at many key inflection points along the path-to-purchase.

All of these opportunities are fairly well understood, but the potential presented by traditional media will soon be changing, giving marketers a significantly greater level of insight into their targets and, as a result, specificity in their messaging. That is because we are at the dawn of the era of addressable broadcast media.

While some content distributors claim that they offer addressable media today[16]—including Cablevision and DirecTV—the current capabilities are rudimentary compared to what will soon be available. Presently, where addressable media is available, marketers can target audiences based on various criteria, including family size and income, enabling different advertising content to be delivered to different homes viewing the same programming at the same time.[17, 18] In the not-too-distant future, a richer range of targeting will be available—and the messaging will be built dynamically at the moment of viewing, as many online advertising campaigns are, delivering customized offers, imagery, calls to action, and other content based on a variety of more powerful and sophisticated audience criteria, including search history, social likes, and recent purchases.

Broadcast commercials and pre-roll video streaming will essentially become one-to-one media vehicles. When it is raining in a local market, for example, the broadcast or pre-roll messaging for umbrellas could focus on the umbrella's unique features for someone who recently searched the category, the umbrella's look and designer provenance for a fashion-conscious clothes-hound, or a special low price for the viewer who tends to explore the entire store when driven to a retail location. If the messaging is from a retailer, the same spot could feature a different brand of umbrella for each viewer based on each one's unique purchasing history and brand preferences.

Perhaps most powerfully of all, marketers will have the ability to address each individual at the key points before, during, and after their transaction with messaging tailored to their unique interests and path-to-purchase. In other words, the capabilities inherent in addressable broadcast would give marketers the opportunity to create more value for both the viewer and the marketer with each piece of communication. There will always be limits, of course. As data and targeting capabilities grow to enable marketers to become more and more precise in their messaging, it will be critical that marketers focus on creating experiences that their users perceive as valuable rather than overly familiar to the point of being off-putting. That is the situation Target found itself in with their addressable mailer when they discovered through data mining that a teenage shopper was pregnant before her father had discovered the same fact.[19, 20]

Regardless of technology, activating behaviors that drive toward transaction will always require understanding the true needs and wants of the shopper, and identifying the brand's best opportunities to satisfy them.

THE CASE FOR RADIO

Somewhere between 91% and 93% of all Americans listen to broadcast radio in a week[21, 22] mostly away from home. As a medium, it is localized, it is immediate, and it offers a wide variety of formats to reach a highly qualified audience.[23]

In many ways, it is the ultimate direct response medium. Heavy radio listeners spend the most time online, more than heavy television viewers and heavy print users. They have the second-highest household incomes (with print users being the highest), and they spend the most amount of time on social media among the three groups.[24]

Welcome to radio, the medium that has been dying, according to pundits, since the invention of television.[25]

Clearly, radio is alive and well—and evolving. From a brand-activation standpoint, radio can be used effectively to drive consumers online to explore a brand, just as it can be the timely extra push right before a purchase. On top of it all, it can play as pivotal a role in helping to build a brand as it can in building its business. Nalley Pickles, a regional brand in the Northwest, did just that with a radio campaign that transformed it from a brand rapidly losing sales to the most popular brand on the market. Most interestingly, during the radio campaign, whenever competitors ran a television spot, viewers credited it to Nalley, helping the brand to increase its perceived stature along with its sales. Tellingly, when the radio campaign was discontinued, the brand lost its first-place status.

Many of the activation opportunities discussed for broadcast television can be applied to radio as well, particularly its power in brand storytelling and driving immediate consumer/shopper engagement. Unique to terrestrial radio in particular, however, are benefits including the ability to update campaigns and executions within short time frames and limited production budgets, opportunities for the station's on-air personalities to endorse the brand, the ability to utilize station staff for "boots on the ground" at local events, and the chance to gain additional presence via station websites and social media channels.

Along with out of home, radio efforts are among the last messages a shopper will experience before making a transaction, providing one of the final chances to impact a purchase decision. Since radio production is also relatively inexpensive, messages can be frequently and easily updated to retain relevance and tie to local current events.

As is the case with broadcast television, Internet radio's ability to target is increasing to the point that it, too, will soon become a one-to-one medium. In the meantime, it gives marketers the ability to gauge response rates through immediate clicks, providing real-time feedback on each spot's effectiveness. Marketers can use this capability to test messaging and calls to action before running a campaign more broadly on terrestrial radio. In addition, Internet radio enables brands to access highly engaged audiences. Merely by the selection of formats and locations—let alone other targeting capabilities—the brand is able to convey their unique values, offers, and calls to action, and align them with listeners.

STILL IN PRINT

There is no disputing the fact that print circulation is declining.[26] Print, however, can still be a very effective medium for appropriate brands with outstanding activation potential. Magazines are highly targeted, so there is very little waste. Their audience is highly engaged and tends to be affluent and educated. The content, even the advertising, is relevant, and people tend to trust print advertising more than television and radio. More importantly, unlike other media, magazine readers welcome advertising—and in some cases, such as wedding books, it might even be *the* reason a person bought the title. What other form of advertising do consumers consistently and intentionally save, let alone collect?

Print advertising's power in driving activation can include delivering new product usage ideas that suggest ways consumers can increase their consumption of the brand's products and, as a result, need to repurchase them with greater frequency. Print can invite prospects to engage in an experience and/or drive them to visit a website. It can also serve as a reminder pre-purchase, as well as a reassurance after a purchase.

While print is obviously paper-based, it is still experiencing numerous innovations, giving marketers new opportunities to activate behaviors. In a 2014 report for FIPP, the global association of magazine publishers, called "Proof of Performance," Guy Consterdine chronicled several recent print advertising innovations, from edible ads that can actually enable flavor sampling to the use of new in-ad technologies. Examples cited included a print ad for Nivea sunscreen that functioned as a phone battery charger through a solar panel embedded in the ad that enabled readers to stay at the beach longer—reinforcing a key brand attribute—and a printed insert for Microsoft Office 365 that turned into its own Wi-Fi hotspot.[27] What's more, as printing technology evolves and variable printing continues to take hold, as it has with direct-response mailings, magazines can also function as a one-to-one medium that enables marketers to more precisely match their messaging with readers' likes and interests, making each ad even more relevant.

As many of these and other examples demonstrate, marketers can effectively use print as an activation vehicle, creating engagement, empowering word of mouth, and inspiring consumers to take an action—while concurrently communicating a brand's values and higher meaning. As a result, if print can reach a marketer's audiences at a key point along their paths-to-purchase, it is a medium that still warrants active consideration.

OUT OF HOME, IN ACTION

When it comes to a long-standing advertising medium, the oldest, in fact, nothing is more suited for activation than out of home (also known as outdoor or billboard advertising). At 99%, it reaches more consumers every week than every other medium, with the time viewing it second only to television.[28] As we continue to spend more and more time in our cars or on public transportation, out of home shows no signs of losing its power.[29]

As an Arbitron National In-Car Study noted, "Billboard advertising is one of the last messages a consumer receives before making a buy decision. Nearly three-quarters of billboard viewers shop on their way home from work; more than two-thirds make their shopping decisions while in the car, and more than one-third make the decision to stop at the store *while* on their way home—all times when billboard advertising has the opportunity to be influential."

The report also noted that out-of-home messages are not only being seen by consumers, but are being acted upon, driving engagement and retail traffic: "Nearly one-quarter of billboard viewers say they were motivated to visit a particular store that day because of an outdoor ad message, and nearly one-third visited a retailer they saw on a billboard later that week. . . . And one-quarter said they immediately visited a business because of an outdoor ad message."

Out-of-home advertising can also be a strong influence on mobile behavior. In fact, within thirty minutes prior to going online, out of home reached approximately 42% of mobile shoppers, 34% of consumers engaged in mobile "brand-related social," and 32% of all mobile search.

Clearly, out of home can be utilized as an effective medium for activating behaviors, and has the potential to be employed along many of the points on a consumer's path-to-purchase. As marketers gain insights into the unique paths taken by their consumers and shoppers, they can optimize their messaging for each point along that path to maximize effectiveness. Additionally, as digital technology continues to evolve, enabling greater interaction between mobile devices and out-of-home vehicles, the targeting and engagement opportunities will only increase, ensuring that the world's first advertising medium will maintain its power and relevance in the modern world.

BUILDING BRAND AND BUILDING BUSINESS

With the world of activation so frequently associated with emerging forms of communications, such as digital and experiential, a reader may wonder why we have used the last several pages to explain and, in some instances, make the case for what has been called *traditional media*. The reason is that effective brand activation requires a perspective that is marketing discipline—and media channel—agnostic, open to any and all potential forms of communication, no matter how new or old, as long as they can be effectively and efficiently utilized to reach and engage consumers and help drive them toward transaction.

Each marketer needs to resist conventional wisdom and one-size-fits-all approaches to methodically identify the optimal media schedule for his or her brand, and remember that it is the overall culmination of interactions with the various communications and experiences that will define the brand, build the image, and—properly applied to align with consumers' purchase paths—change behavior and drive transactions.

The old "rule of three"[30]—that consumers simply need to be exposed to a message three or more times for it to be effective—never really was the case. In fact, research indicates that wear-in is almost immediate—and wear-out happens quickly thereafter.[31] In other words, it is not the repetition of trumpeting the same advertising message over and over again that builds a brand; rather, it is the consistency of conveying the same personality, attitudes, values, associations, promises, and purpose, using an associated and systematically applied tone of voice and set of visual brand elements across all touchpoints, that builds the brand. As for building the business, messaging that does not inspire behavior change by driving consumers along a path-to-purchase does not become effective with repeat showings under the guise of creating attitude change.[32] It never has, and it never will.

In developing their branded programs and messaging, marketers can create engagement with traditional media vehicles through entertainment value, but they also need to be careful not to make messaging too entertaining.

Think of it as an inverse U-shape for effectiveness.[33] Not enough entertainment, and the interactions will be boring; too much, and the marketing message can get lost. The goal is to find the sweet spot, and that sweet spot might evolve as the brand moves through its life cycle.

As advertising and promotions guru Gerald J. Tellis reminds us, "informative appeals are more important early than late in a product's life cycle," while emotional appeals are more effective late rather than early in a product's life cycle."[34]

While effectively achieving brand activation will take fine-tuning, marketers should not be too fast to change their fundamental brand strategy, vision, or visual elements. Brand guru David Aaker identified five factors that might lead a marketer to change a brand: 1) "the brand strategy is poorly conceived"; 2) it's "not breaking through the clutter"; 3) "fundamental changes in the marketplace"; 4) "the business strategy might evolve or even change"; and 5) "the brand and offering may lack energy and visibility."[35]

Each of these reasons comes with several caveats that should be carefully considered first, and Aaker suggests that fixing or adjusting the marketing programs designed to activate the brand might produce better, and perhaps even more profitable, results.

A FEW BRIEF WORDS ON BRIEFING

When initiating a brand-activation program that will encompass broadcast, print, out of home, or radio (as well as any other media vehicles), the brand's essence, mission, vision, values, and personality need to be clearly conveyed in the brief to the creative teams. These elements will become the first critical screens through which marketers must judge the resulting work.

Additionally, the brief needs to precisely define both the consumer and the shopper, convey where all messaging falls on their paths-to-purchase, and identify the program's key performance indicators, so all stakeholders are aligned on how the work will be evaluated when in market. These parameters will then need to be applied as key screens in evaluating any and all potential ideas or directions.

Finally, and perhaps most importantly, the initial focus should be on developing the overall activation idea, and then, based on the program and its opportunities to help consumers or shoppers over their key inflection points, the messaging and approach to the supporting traditional advertising vehicles can follow. For some, this sequence will be a revolutionary change from the long-standing practice of developing a mass media messaging campaign first and then extending it to the other channels, but if the goal is brand activation, this approach will increase the campaign's cohesiveness, resonance, and effectiveness.

Brands will always need to define themselves in the marketplace by communicating to prospects what they mean and the values they represent, and traditional media vehicles remain powerful ways to do that, as well as to activate consumer behaviors. Actions, however, speak louder than words, particularly when those actions align with key prospects' paths-to-purchase. That is the key thought behind the AIM—utilizing even the most traditional of media vehicles to not only telegraph what the brand stands for, but to also create engagement that drives those it is designed to reach closer to a transaction.

There is one area of marketing completely focused on understanding and making the most of the shopper's journey. Why has it become so powerful, and how can it be better leveraged by marketers? Find out in the next chapter.

4

Start with the Shopper (Marketing)

Is a beloved brand truly beloved if nobody buys it? That is the question marketers have to ask themselves if their brands score high on likability, intention to buy, and other metrics that indicate audiences understand and love their brands' stories, but the brands are not winning the battle for transactions.

Of course, consumers need to understand and like a brand. But to ultimately triumph at the register, marketers need to successfully activate their brands in and around their retail environments, and that requires knowing who is shopping and buying the brands, as well as how they are shopped and bought.

It is precisely these insights that are the unique expertise of retail/shopper marketing, and it is this marketing discipline that will be the focus of this chapter.

Awareness-focused media advertising can move a brand into the consideration set, but in most product and service categories shoppers tend to have more than one brand they may be considering. What happens from there is dependent on the shopping experience, and the selection and deselection process employed by each individual shopper.

Within virtually every category there are brands that have their unwaveringly fervent loyalists; just consider Coke and Pepsi, for example (or McDonald's and Burger King, BMW and Mercedes-Benz, Nike and Adidas, etc.). Shifting a loyal Coke drinker to Pepsi is highly unlikely, just as is the other way around. Where the battleground lies, however, is in targeting the individuals who can go either way, whether it is because they do not perceive the brand differences as meaningful, their needs and desires are changing, or because they have just entered the category and have not yet developed a strong affiliation with one brand or the other. You may even be one of them.

Maybe you love the taste of Coke, but Pepsi is okay, too, and you drink it once in a while. You love the latest Coca-Cola ad campaign and what it represents, while Pepsi runs a steady and consistent stream of advertising you perceive as just okay. What the brand stands for to you is not bad, just not great. So while you do not love it, you will not be embarrassed being seen with it, either. On a given day, you stop in to a convenience store on your way to an appointment to grab a Coke, but Pepsi's new packaging catches your attention, and it is on special at a great deal. It has an eye-catching display that offers you the chance to win tickets to a long-sold-out concert you had been dreaming of attending. Which brand is more likely to get purchased by someone in your situation? Yes: Pepsi.

MARKETING AT THE DECISION POINT
Welcome to the power of shopper marketing (also called "retail marketing," particularly when the marketer controls the retail channel). It is where a slightly more compelling and well-timed message delivered by an often-hard-won presence strategically close to the point of transaction can be the difference that results in big profits. One of the perennially innovative leaders in the practice, Procter & Gamble, increased sales of their beauty products by more than 58%, and exceeded their sales goals by 40%, simply by eliminating their one-size-fits-all retail approach and replacing it with micro-programs that better aligned with how women typically shop the category in each of their top retailers.[1]

Shopper marketing's deep insights into the behaviors throughout the purchase process—and unique ability to create critical advantages over competitors along the way—make it one of the key strategic underpinnings for the AIM by helping to enable the more-effective alignment of all of the marketing specialties. If each component of a program is focused just a bit more precisely on addressing the key shopping behavior barriers and opportunities, it is easy to understand how the resulting increase in sales impact can be meaningful.

The world of shopper marketing and its battle to actually close the transactions that are the ultimate goal of every marketing plan is high-stakes and deceptively complex, which may help to explain why it is so widely misunderstood and so commonly associated with in-store messaging. As practiced by the most sophisticated marketers in the space, including Coca-Cola and Procter & Gamble, shopper marketing fully leverages the complex interrelationship and codependencies that exist between the shopper, the retailer, and the brand to create wins for all.

More specifically, as the goal is to ultimately create a situation where the marketer's brand wins the transaction battle over its competitors, the brand needs to win with the shopper by optimally delivering the right message at the right time and in the right way during each shopper's path-to-purchase. Winning with the shopper, however, typically requires winning with the retailer in order to enable the presence and engagement opportunities so critical to reaching the shopper at their key inflection points. Winning with the shopper, winning with the retailer, and ultimately creating wins for the brand each require a unique set of strategies, tools, tactics, and approaches that quickly increase the complexity for the marketer and are best understood by analyzing the intersection points between two at a time.

Before we dive in, however, it is important to point out that while discussions on shopper marketing are often focused on situations where the brand does not control the retail environment (i.e., Procter & Gamble and Coca-Cola, in that there are no "P&G stores," and they are largely dependent on the likes of Target and Walmart), when the brand is the retailer (i.e., Starbucks and many B2B marketers), "winning with the retailer" means delivering winning executions at the key points of influence within an individual retail environment (such as proper program and messaging executions within the local Starbucks on the corner, or during the sales presentation in a specific distributor's showroom).

As will become clear in the coming pages, all marketers can benefit from these shopper marketing principles, even if their applications may vary. Here are the basic key principles:

- Each shopper follows his/her own nonlinear path-to-purchase (which is why many of the most sophisticated practitioners in the space actually go so far as to create shopper segmentations in addition to consumer segmentations).
- Winning with the retailer requires understanding their unique retailer brand and objectives in order to craft win-win scenarios for both the marketer and

the retailer (which often requires reconciling manufacturer and retailer segmentations of their key strategic targets to enable collaboration).

- Winning for the brand can often require truly co-branded programs between manufacturers and retailers (which are quickly evolving beyond
one-off account-specific programs into complete co-branded calendars of
activities).

As is usually the case, and a lesson the marketing world at large can learn
from its retail marketing brethren, the best place to begin is with the shopper.

UNDERSTANDING SHOPPING GOALS AND BEHAVIORS

In chapter 2, we began to discuss the important reality that the shopper and
consumer are not always the same individual; in fact, their interests and motivations may be quite different. For example, the consumer may be looking
for status, while the shopper might want to save money. Or, conversely, the
consumer may simply be interested in the utility of a product, while the shopper is motivated to show they care by purchasing a recognized name brand.

Even when the shopper and consumer are the same individual, however, it
is critical to be mindful that the shopping mind-set is fundamentally different
from the consuming mind-set. The former is a process of selection and deselection, while the latter is an experience of the selected product's utility and
rational/emotional value, or lack thereof. This insight holds true whether the
brand controls the retail environment, such as at a quick service restaurant,
or the brand is being sold through another retail brand's environment, such
as with a packaged-goods product at a grocery store. It is true whether the
shopper is in a brick-and-mortar channel or shopping online, and it is true
across all types of products and services, from the consumer world to B2B.

To best understand the shopper's mind-set and behaviors, marketers need
to begin with the point of transaction,[2] which Procter & Gamble—and possibly
their chairman, A. G. Lafley—identified as the "first moment of truth,"[3, 4] and
work backwards from there. By tracing the shopper's journey in reverse, from
point of purchase to the journey's initiation, marketers can identify the many
forking paths that represent the myriad unique routes shoppers take, and identify where brand-activation activities would be most helpful and, most importantly, why. These insights will become the foundational building blocks of the
marketer's broader activation efforts to follow.

Just as an individual's consuming and shopping mind-sets differ, so, too, do the individual's mind-sets while shopping different types of retail channels. A shopper would not typically be in stock-up mode at a convenience store—just as he or she would not usually run to a wholesale club solely to pick up a single carton of milk. Because these channel-based shopper mind-sets are different, the visit expectations are also different, and because the expectations are different, the opportunities and challenges for both the shopper and marketer are necessarily different as well.

Consider an iPhone shopper and how the shopper's information requests, openness to add-on purchases, expectations of service (or savings), and more will vary greatly between the "Genius Bar" at a shopping mall Apple store, the Apple e-commerce site, a brick-and-mortar cell-phone store, and a big box retailer, whether online or off.

Understanding the shopper's specific goal(s) and behaviors within each channel can lead to insights that increase the effectiveness of a marketing program, not just in the immediate sales situation, but further back along the purchase path as well.

Does the shopper need to get in and out fast, or have more time to explore; expect a lower price, or expect one-to-one sales help? Will the shopper use a mobile device in-store for price comparisons, or research the product/service before entering the retail environment? Or is the retail visit itself the research, with the shopper making the actual transaction via mobile in their car following the visit?

The answers will lead marketers to a better understanding of the needs and expectations along the different paths-to-purchase, enabling a more seamless omni-channel approach that effectively integrates online, mobile, and in-store opportunities into an ownable brand experience optimized for each sales channel.

Marketers will find these insights important not just when creating marketing programs across retailers, but also within each retailer. Consider, for example, all of the different retail channels under the Walmart banner: from Supercenters to small-format stores, from Neighborhood Markets to Walmart To Go, and, of course, Walmart.com. Properly utilized, each of these channels can lead to greater profitability for the brand, as well as greater satisfaction for both the shopper and the consumer.

The bleeding edge in the shopper/retail marketing space is the development of shopper segmentations to capture the unique paths key groups of shoppers are taking on their journey toward transaction. Consider the makeup shopper who samples products with the white-coated skin-care experts in the department store, only to then search for the desired product at a discount online and brag about her savvy purchase on Facebook (or via a haul video on YouTube). She follows a path that is very different from her girlfriend, who hears about the product when it is shared on Facebook, along with many other products her friends have raved about, researches all of them via style bloggers online, and ultimately buys the one she chooses at Target while back-to-school shopping for her kids. Both women may have even walked right by their ultimately selected product while it was on sale at their local pharmacy, because they were in their caregiver mind-set, focused on their mission of picking up prescriptions for their families and never considering the drugstore a personal beauty products destination.

Even understanding who uses social media for opinion research early in the shopping process versus those who use it to share raves post-purchase, or who is open to what types of shopping in what retail channels, can result in very different communications, offers, and activation programs, not to mention retailer partnerships, sponsorships, and sampling events. In the same way that marketers for decades have created consumer segments and utilized them in targeting, so now marketers can utilize shopper segments to not only prioritize targeting by retail channel, but to also sequence or even customize messaging by segment. As all marketing continues its transition from mass media to one-to-one engagement, thanks to uniquely identifiable digital communication channels, there may be as many segments as there are shoppers, which will be discussed further in the mass micro-personalization section of chapter 7 on direct/database marketing.

THE INSIGHTS TO WIN WITHIN RETAIL ENVIRONMENTS

It is not just shopping behavior and the product or service brand that today's marketers need to consider and understand; they also need insight into their retailers' brands—particularly if the product or service brand is not the same brand as the point of distribution. In fact, understanding the retailer's brand and priorities is key to designing effective programs and achieving retailer participation in them, whether they are national programs, account-specific, co-branded efforts, or fully collaborative marketing calendars. After all, it should come as no surprise that the retailer is only concerned with the brand's

FIGURE 4.1
Winning efforts leverage the intersection of shopper, retail, and brand insights.
Source: Designed by Sarah Vonderhaar.

shoppers who buy at their retail locations and, as a result, with how the brand can help the retailer advance his or her priorities and vision.

Marketers are best served by thinking of retail marketing as a Venn diagram, and striving to find and understand the intersections between the shopper insights, retailer insights, and brand insights. Winning efforts will leverage the common ground between all three, because they will enable the marketer to develop a program based on the interests and priorities of the retailer, that engages and attracts the target shopper, and brings the brand to life in a way that is consistent with its positioning and vision. Finding that intersection will also enable a more-effective sequencing of messaging, and, ultimately, more-engaging and better-executed programs, which will create more opportunities to cross-sell, upsell, and bounce back, whether it is across pages and clicks or doors and aisles.

This same approach applies to B2B marketers selling in environments such as industry trade shows. The marketer needs to understand the brand promise and unique experience of the show, along with the needs and interests of the attendees, in addition to the relevant attributes of their brand. Many marketers, however, frequently deploy one-size-fits-all approaches in these environments, often overlooking the brand-development priorities of the trade show, leading to conflicting agendas and missed opportunities.

Imagine if the promise of a trade show is on creating better, more-productive environments. If a marketer developed an activation program to drive booth traffic and prospect engagement that also creates a better environment at the trade show itself, one could imagine tremendous support and potentially increased executional latitude from the show's organizers. The trade show would be provided with a way to better demonstrate and fulfill its promise to attendees, which in turn could create potential leverage for the marketer to negotiate a higher profile for their brand within the environment, and/or preferred pricing for executing a program that is perceived as a win-win.

GET IN THE ZONE(S)

All marketers, from those who control their retail environments to those who are looking to close transactions in environments managed by others, need to understand the path their shoppers take within it, physically, rationally, and emotionally. What do prospects typically see and experience first, second, and third in the environment? How long do they spend where? What are they trying to accomplish and where do they focus their attention? When they enter, are they searching for a department or a shopping cart? Are they reading the menu or looking for the shortest line? Understanding the unique nuances of the shopper journey and the many behavioral zones that can exist within a retail environment can help marketers to more effectively tell their brand story, identify optimal locations for communications and interaction, and fully leverage opportunities to achieve cross-sell, add-on, or trade-up purchases.

These areas and opportunities, of course, extend across both online and physical environments. As shoppers routinely cross between the online and off-line worlds—and often inhabit both at once, such as when they are utilizing their smartphones in-aisle—so strategies and approaches must cross on- and off-line as well. Crate and Barrel, for example, lifted their online sales by 44% simply by observing how consumers shopped in their physical stores and then mirroring that approach in their online navigation.[5] Whether the opportunity is to place a chilled single-serve soda at the cash wrap for a shopper to enjoy on the ride home or to merchandise a loyalty program on the order confirmation that offers a discount on a return visit, when executed properly, the result can be happier shoppers and incremental sales.

When marketers control the retail environment, they can manage messaging across the entire experience to optimize the visit from ingress to egress. Just as a product on a shelf needs to be visible among all of the others, so the retail environment itself needs to stand out and be easy to locate and access. Exterior messaging needs to not just aid in way-finding, but should also deliver relevant news to drive traffic. Within the environment, way-finding is important to create a satisfying and frictionless experience, as are strategically placed trade-up, add-on, and bounce-back messages. Marketers need to understand not only how consumers travel through the environment, but what information they are looking for, and when, so messaging can be positioned to help them find what they need and achieve their objectives.

If customers get frustrated, they will leave and find what they are looking for elsewhere, as cart abandonment is not just an e-commerce issue, but a brick-and-mortar one as well. But when shoppers are enabled and appropriately engaged in any environment, they stay longer and shop more, which can result in increased sales as they recall additional items they need, or discover new items they never knew they needed. At the close of the journey, the messaging should invite the shoppers to return by planting the seed of a reason to do so, which can be leveraged in future follow-up communication opportunities.

Understanding the shopper's journey, of course, also enables the marketer to convey their brand's story in a way that is most relevant to the shopper, bringing to life its key core attributes and reflecting the most relevant aspects of its brand essence at the right times. Likewise, B2B marketers need to understand how prospects travel through their retail environments and trade show experiences. What can be done on the exterior via messaging and design to capture attention and gain interest? How can messaging and programs drive prospects deeper into the booth area to enhance engagement and commitment? What data can be gleaned, and when, to help focus the conversation on the most salient sales points? The answers to these questions and the resulting opportunities and actions will in themselves generate improved brand activation and return on investment.

THE ENTIRE PACKAGE

An often under-leveraged communication vehicle that is of particular relevance to consumer packaged goods (CPG) marketers is packaging. Whether the marketer approaches the package itself as an extension of their branding efforts, their retail marketing efforts, their content marketing (since the marketer "owns" and "publishes" it), or all three, the packaging cannot be divorced from the environment(s) in which the brand is being sold. After all, if a package does not capture attention at the point of purchase and deliver the communications relevant to closing the sale, it will not be noticed or it will not be bought, and most likely both.

Marketers have to assume that the packaging is the only messaging a shopper will view, because it just may be, as more and more retailers move to clean store policies designed to reduce manufacturer presence and messaging. Of course, as much as a brand's identity, the packaging has to convey the brand and its promise, while also being easy to find and understand. Shoppers tend to search for products by the packaging's shapes, imagery, and colors, which can also be important to communicating its taste profiles or features. As a result, packaging must not only facilitate discovery and navigation within product variations, but it must also single-handedly communicate the brand's positioning in relation to other brands within the category and, if needed, provide usage ideas, instructions, and more.

Marketers, however, need to be cautious and strategic in evolving their packaging and plan for pre-change messaging signaling the impending modifications, so as not to alienate current consumers. There have been sufficient examples of spectacular missteps in this area to encourage abundant caution, such as Tropicana's failed package change in 2009 when sales plummeted 20%.[6] They all serve as reminders to marketers to utilize shopper and retailer insights to optimize not only their packaging but their mix of stock keeping units (SKUs), ensuring the right sizes, features, and messages for the right shoppers and environments, which alone can produce a noticeable increase in shopper acceptance and sales volume.

NEW SCHOOL, OLD SCHOOL

No discussion of shopper/retail marketing would be complete without addressing the increasing role that technology plays and can play in all aspects of the shopper's experience. E-commerce and mobile commerce capabilities have increased the potential points of purchase to such a degree that marketers more and more need to treat every environment as a retail environment. To that end, and perhaps more importantly, new technologies continue to expand the ways that consumers can interact with brands and receive information and value along their paths-to-purchase. Through the strategic use of geofencing or beacon technology, marketers can send an alert to shoppers when they approach, enter, or travel through a store, providing a friendly reminder—and even an incentive—to restock a favorite brand or perhaps try a new one, based on a personalized recommendation.[7] Alternatively, a marketer can simply provide a store map or other relevant visit information that can make the shopper's experience more productive and enjoyable.

Regardless of approach, the shopper data these technologies create are immensely powerful. As a result, shopper loyalty programs continue to improve as checkout scanners link to shopper databases and can be used to not just deliver a bounce-back offer on a shopper's receipt via Catalina's platform, but also to trigger instant offers at the point of sale, deliver points toward future rewards, or be leveraged into a timed e-mail or direct-mail communication designed to entice the shopper back into the aisles more quickly.

As the pace of innovation and technology options increase, marketers need to pay close attention to what shoppers will find helpful and valuable—and what they will not. Interactive kiosks and the scanning of QR codes, for example, were never widely adopted by the vast majority of shoppers and are quickly being forgotten, because the time and effort they required did not produce significant shopper value. Similarly, marketers have to be careful not to be too quick to drop the tried-and-true in favor of the new and shiny. For instance, while shoppers are adopting Groupon and other social deal tactics, they continue to utilize long-established strategies, such as coupons and sale periods, to stock up on regularly purchased items at a discount. As long as shoppers continue to find these types of programs valuable and motivating, marketers need to continue creating and leveraging them, even as they nurture what may be their future replacements.

GETTING DOWN TO BUSINESS-TO-BUSINESS

Understanding the science of shopper marketing can help B2B marketers beyond just enhancing their lead-generation results at yearly trade show events. B2B marketers need to understand their prospects' journey toward transaction and how to activate it to enhance ROI as much as their consumer counterparts.

B2B marketers should also start at the end of the path-to-purchase and focus initially on the point of transaction—in their case, the final capabilities presentation and contract negotiation—and then work their way back up the path to the initial point of business need and brand awareness. Often an important point to consider along that path is the brand's website. How do prospects travel through it, and how long do they stay? Consider their path from page to page. Does it make sense, or are they spending too much time in one section or another because they may be confused or not finding the information they need? When do prospects typically leave the site, and from what page? Utilizing these basic web analytics can be enlightening, as in many ways a B2B website can be a virtual store environment or even product packaging, because it is the vehicle that has to both clearly convey the brand and ultimately play a critical role in helping to make the sale.

B2B marketers, of course, also need to look further upstream and understand the paths to receiving the initial inquiry or request for proposal (RFP). Do prospects typically find the brand online by searching the category and then landing on an infographic, white paper, or other piece of content marketing? Or do they often discover it at a trade show, after receiving an e-mail, or by other means? The order of contacts that a group of prospects tends to utilize along their path to transaction can be segmented into types, just as with consumers. Those segmentations may even go so far as to include the internal organizational dynamics required to approve a supplier purchase. For example, is the organization one with a single decision maker, or several? If the latter, what are their interrelationships, sequences of involvement, and varying priorities? For example, is the procurement department the first point of contact or the last, once the field is narrowed?

The more information the marketer can have about the prospect and the path ahead, the better the messages and points of contact can be managed to move a potential buyer more quickly toward transaction. As insight grows, logical groupings of organization types and their corresponding paths will often emerge and can be leveraged to increase effectiveness and efficiency.

CHECKOUT POWER

Once the brand marketer fully understands the shoppers' paths-to-purchase and the opportunities to create wins within key retail touchpoints, more-effective activation programs can then be developed, capitalizing on select opportunities to drive trade-up and add-on purchases via offers, experiences, or sponsorships that engage the shopper and enhance the brand experience. Consider these examples:

Walmart and Coca-Cola provided a powerful instance of shopper marketing with their co-branded program focused on changing dinner planning from a shopping list to a menu. Their collaborative, co-branded effort was built upon three key insights into their mutually targeted shopper segment: 1) Coke is this shopper's desired beverage at dinner,[8] 2) Walmart's deli department was not seen as a destination or reason to visit for this shopper,[9] and 3) 57% of dinners are planned and purchased within an hour before mealtime.[10] Together, Coca-Cola and Walmart launched a program called "Effortless Meals at Walmart," turning the dinner shopping list into a ready-to-serve-and-eat menu by jointly promoting complete, preprepared meals available at the Walmart deli counter.

Through the creation of these one-stop bundles for the convenience-seeking shopper, Coke gained valuable merchandising and incremental product presence at Walmart's deli counters. In return, Coke extended their Coke Rewards points to include Walmart deli purchases, adding the kind of value Walmart and its shoppers crave.[11]

The program leveraged the insight into last-minute dinner planning and buying behavior by promoting the offer during the key three-to-five p.m. day-part using channels that would reach shoppers at key decision points along their path-to-purchase, including radio and gas station TV to reach those already in their cars, and through targeted broadcast television and digital messaging on relevant sites and Facebook to reach those not yet on their way. Perhaps more importantly for Coca-Cola, the program also received branded presence in-store at Walmart (an environment that is said to generate more exposure in a week than any commercial on any single television show), reaching dinner shoppers prepurchase via merchandising in and around the deli counter. As a result, according to *Chief Marketer*'s report on the 2014 Pro Awards, Coca-Cola sales grew by 3.6% at Walmart to the benefit of both, beating their goal of 2% growth and reversing a drop in sales of 5% the previous year.[12]

Another revealing example comes from Kraft Heinz Canada. Kraft Heinz had high awareness among millennial mothers in Canada, but was experiencing steep sales declines versus the rest of the category due to the target's impression of their products as highly processed and old-fashioned. To help counter that trend, Kraft Heinz leveraged another trend known as "food hacking," where millennial cooks utilize familiar ingredients in new, innovative ways. Food-hacking recipe ideas were created that required just three easy steps and were explained via compelling infographics, with each step spotlighting a different Kraft Heinz product. Food-hack recipes were customized by account to best align with the goals and objectives of key retailers, and were communicated at key inflection points including via in-store displays that featured the mentioned products, direct mail to those in the Kraft What's Cooking database, print ads in relevant publications, social media, and a website where consumers could share their own video creations featuring their food hacks. Across all of these touchpoints, Kraft Heinz adopted a more modern and relevant Pinterest-esque look and feel for their communications, featuring less selling copy and a more visual and telegraphic design approach.

By aligning the needs and desires of the shopper, the retailer, and the brand, the program achieved a sales increase of over 11%, more than double the goal, as well as engagement levels that more than tripled baseline averages, with stores that participated enjoying a 41% increase in unit sales over stores that did not.[13] Not bad for a group of dated brands including Jell-O, Miracle Whip, and Kraft dressings, trying to activate the highly elusive millennial audience.

AIM BIGGER

The principles and best practices of shopper/retail marketing are a key component of any and all brand-activation efforts. Without insight into shoppers' behaviors and the ability to win within a retail environment, marketers lose the ability to drive transactions, and even worse, may be driving consumers to the point of purchase only to hand them over to the competition right before they reach the register.

As digital technologies have enabled literally anywhere and everywhere to become a retail environment, it is critical that marketers construct their activation efforts utilizing the key foundational elements of shopper/retail marketing effectiveness, including the following:

- Each shopper follows his/her own unique nonlinear path-to-purchase.
- Winning with a retailer's shoppers requires understanding the retailer's unique brand and objectives in order to craft win-win scenarios for both the marketer and the retailer when they are not one and the same.
- Winning for the marketer's brand can often require co-branded programs between manufacturer and retailer, as demonstrated by the Coca-Cola and Walmart example.

As discussed in chapter 2, the learnings and tools that originated in shopper marketing have applicability beyond what is most narrowly defined as retail, and can be powerful when more broadly applied in marketers' activation efforts.

As a result, segmenting shoppers and not just consumers, understanding how shopper mind-sets and behaviors can change across retail channels, and diagnosing and addressing key behavioral inflection points along the path-to-purchase are all foundational aspects of applying the AIM.

The next arena within which to gain insights and leverage previously fragmented tools is the very point where consumers and shoppers spend more and more of their time today—online, on their phones, and on social media. Join us for the next chapter as we explore how to fully leverage the unique opportunities they represent and the role they can play when applying the AIM.

5

Connecting with Digital, Social, and Mobile

In any discussion of digital media, it is important to acknowledge that what is currently referred to as "digital" has become so fundamental to today's marketing efforts as to render the term nearly meaningless. Virtually all marketing today is either digital, digitally enabled, or digitally connected to such a degree that maybe a better term would simply be "marketing." Shortly we will no longer be talking about digital as some sort of separate or specialized area, but instead a foundational enabler of all efforts. That said, to not devote some focused time to the depth and breadth of digital marketing, and to mobile and social in particular, would be to understate its power and importance in connecting with consumers and shoppers, and in activating brands.

To that end, this chapter will address how to take full advantage of the tremendous activation capabilities and opportunities presented by websites, online advertising, mobile apps, paid and organic search, digital content, social media platforms, e-commerce, m-commerce (via smartphones), t-commerce (via smart televisions), and more. All offer today's marketer myriad opportunities to activate behavior and deliver engaging, branded experiences that create value for people as they move through their daily lives and their multiple, nonlinear paths-to-purchase.

Within the digital universe, mobile is currently a subset and refers to the ability of consumers to access all of the above while not tethered to their desktop devices. This, at present, means smartphones, tablets, and wearables, but it is critical to understand that mobile is quickly becoming the center of the digital universe, as evidenced by the steady increase in smartphone penetration, from 20% in 2010 to almost two-thirds of Americans forecast to own a smartphone in 2017.[1] For many demographics, a mobile device is already the primary connection to the digital world.

In other words, just as all marketing is becoming digital, all digital is becoming mobile.

The importance of this point cannot be overstated for marketers interested in activating brands, as mobile provides unique opportunities and capabilities to engage consumers and help them move toward transactions. These include functionality associated with mobile wallets that can store coupons, tickets, boarding passes, and credit and debit cards that enable frictionless one-click transactions; location awareness that via geofencing, iBeacon, Google Beacon, and near field communication (NFC) can enable "right place/right time" contextual communications and push notifications; and camera and video capabilities that facilitate real-time participation and sharing of experiences. Mobile not only enables marketers to reach each consumer anywhere—and everywhere—along his or her unique path-to-purchase, but also to engage in a true, real-time dialogue, exchanging relevant information, incentives, instructions, invitations, photos, video, and more.

MAKE IT MOBILE

Mobile marketing and m-commerce is clearly changing the ways people shop and buy. Much has been written about showrooming, for example—the practice of experiencing a product in a physical store and then buying it (usually for less) online, sometimes via mobile while still at the retailer.[2] But mobile's power can also enable the dynamic to work both ways, empowering consumers to research products via their phones while in the aisles to facilitate purchasing the item in-store.

Mobile is becoming, if it has not already become, the key conduit through which people are connecting with each other and the world—from managing calendars, finances, and friends and family on social networks, to navigating online, on the road, and on the path-to-purchase. Many marketers, however, to their own detriment, are still treating it as ancillary to their primary marketing efforts.

Unlocking the real potential of mobile requires a shift in mind-set that embraces mobile's full location-aware, transaction-driving power, and views it as the ultimate one-to-one media channel. Mobile gives consumers and marketers the opportunity to engage at every point along a shopper's path-to-purchase—from planning and considering, to comparing, buying, and reviewing—which means opportunities to inspire participation in programs that can create behavior change.

The Montana Office of Tourism made the shift, spending a mere $25,000 on a mobile-based campaign promoting skiing in their state that netted nearly seven million additional tourism dollars. Their impetus was the shopper behavior observation "that skiers are 200 percent more likely than the general population to use their phones to explore and plan trips."[3] Utilizing this insight, the Montana Office of Tourism decided to target prospects with mobile advertising—but their approach went beyond merely placing ads on mobile sites related to skiing, although that can certainly be effective. Rather, they targeted skiers on the slopes, in the shops, and at the outdoor retailers of select cities that were well-attended, competitive ski destinations, but with slopes inferior to what Montana could offer.

The mobile advertising content brought to life the contrast between the skier's current location and the vastly superior ski experience that was available to them in Montana, delivering the right message at the right time to maximize impact, and generating a click-through rate to their website that was four times the travel industry average. Through the use of geofencing technology, which utilizes GPS or radio-frequency identification (RFID) to define virtual geographic boundaries, they surrounded the entire state of Montana and were then able to determine the actual number of mobile ad recipients who subsequently visited the state for a skiing excursion.

The results? They increased attendance by more than 4,700 people, which resulted in a $6.9 million lift in visitor spending and a $276 return for every dollar spent on the campaign—all from strategically utilizing mobile's capabilities.

The Montana example clearly demonstrates the possibilities of using location-aware mobile technology—both in the message delivery to drive behavior change, as well as in the campaign assessment and attribution to quantify results and ROI.

Mobile can also be utilized to immediately drive transactions. Many retailers, and some consumer packaged goods (CPG) manufacturers, are experimenting with beacon technology that enables them to deliver a high-value offer at the moment a shopper nears a promoted item.[4] That content can also be personalized based on data analytics that provide insight into shoppers' preferences and interests, in addition to proximity.[5]

Meaningful incentives and messages can be delivered earlier in the shopper's journey as well, or even after a transaction. The goal for marketers, based on the insights gleaned from understanding shoppers' paths-to-purchase, is to find the most meaningful and valuable inflection points when they can and should communicate with their potential customers. Forrester calls them "Mobile Moments"—the "point in time and place when a consumer pulls out a mobile device to get what she wants immediately, in context."[6] A similar concept is Google's "Moments That Matter," with the managing director of Google UK, Eileen Naughton, declaring that "mobile is a behaviour; we should stop thinking of it as a device."[7]

Whatever the nomenclature, the point is the same. It is hard to find a more powerful vehicle through which to reach shoppers in context than mobile. While messages can certainly be personalized, as mentioned in chapter 3, Forrester reminds us that it is more important to reach people at appropriate times with appropriate messaging. In one of their key takeaways, the authors of the report wrote, "Consumers will view untimely or irrelevant messages as annoying even if the messages are personalized. Initiating a mobile moment at exactly the right time and place is essential to success."[8] In other words, the communication needs to provide some form of immediate and relevant value—whether it is simply helpful information, a financial incentive, or an experiential opportunity. This idea of driving engagement by creating value is a key principle of the AIM whose importance cannot be overstated.

While many of mobile's technical requirements currently force marketers to utilize specialists, a need that should lessen as capabilities advance and digital marketing activities become more aligned, the key to success resides in realizing that mobile's unique activation opportunities come from the confluence of four key marketing disciplines: social, shopper, promotion, and customer relationship management (CRM).

As a one-to-one vehicle, mobile is clearly elevating the role of direct and database marketing, which we will discuss further in chapter 7, as many of the principles and practices are essentially the same. Many even view digital in general, and mobile in particular, as direct marketing "on steroids," because of the immediacy of response and data that it offers, enabling a constant, information-rich interaction with shoppers. Clearly, however, its power to influence purchase decisions is the ultimate payoff.

MOBILE MEETS SHOPPER

From looking up store hours, getting directions, and reading reviews to receiving deals, comparing prices, and actually paying, mobile has the ability to function as an informed shopping assistant, 24/7, and the marketing potential, as a result, is nothing short of staggering. Retailers who simply offer mobile-optimized sites increase consumer engagement by 21%, with 85%[9] of consumers reporting they are more likely to purchase from those retailers, according to a study from Deloitte Digital.

Moving beyond the basics, however, requires tangible insights into consumers' multiple and nonlinear paths-to-purchase. Unfortunately, until that full understanding is achieved, marketers may be focusing their valuable resources on influencing points along the path-to-purchase with lower ROI potential. In fact, Forrester, in their Mobile Moments study, shared findings that currently in the mobile space, the "use of messaging is heaviest upstream where it delivers the least value."[10]

As emphasized in the previous chapter, marketers who do not control their own retail channels need to understand the priorities of their retail partners and work with them to optimize site experiences and apps to deliver what shoppers need, when they need it, including such critical information as how and where to buy, as well as relevant product details when they are needed.

Once those steps are taken, mobile becomes a powerful medium that will be the key to effectively leveraging opportunities represented by beacon technology and near field communications. That is why increasingly, virtually all shopper marketing programs have an overarching digital and related mobile component. It can enable the manufacturer to know precisely which shopper is being reached within which retail partner, and manage their communications accordingly.

CREATE VALUE TO CREATE ENGAGEMENT

Whether it is a website, app, or mobile site, marketers cannot assume that if they build it, consumers will come—not to mention download, engage, opt in, and participate. With hundreds of millions of apps and sites available, marketers' mobile offerings need to incent engagement and deliver real value and utility to drive ongoing participation.

Just compare the number of apps on your phone right now to the number you've actually used in the last month, and the point becomes clear. As a result, branded games, tiered awards, targeted offers, and unique experiences are important to driving both initial trial and, often, ongoing participation. Driving successful mobile or social engagement is the marketing challenge within the marketing challenge, and valuable, branded offers can help.

To create value beyond the monetary, marketers can deliver shoppers and consumers real functional utility, entertainment content, and/or opportunities to participate in something of interest—such as games, contests, photo/video sharing, hashtags, or how-to information—versus merely sending marketing messages and perhaps a coupon.

Even the most basic utility, such as being able to find a clean restroom via Charmin's Sit-Or-Squat mobile app, represents a branded opportunity to demonstrate technology's power to create unexpected value in consumers' daily lives.

In addition to offering participation opportunities, timing is also key to running a successful program, and this requires a shift in how marketers view their delivery. In fact, Forrester, in their Mobile Moments report, points out that "too many business professionals view messaging as a tactic to deliver promotions or updates that drive action later in the week or simply interrupt the day. Too few professionals view messaging as a tool to transform a customer experience with timely information that inspires immediate action."[11] In many situations, that action could involve social platforms, content, or direct engagements with a representative of the brand.

For more and more people, smartphones and tablets are the primary link to their social networks and are fast becoming the preferred choice for social interactions.[12] Mobile is the easiest way to quickly share photos or experiences—from those on the go to those at home. People are not only using it to tweet, check in, and update status; they're also using it to download daily deals, access their networks' brand and product recommendations, and, of course, share their own insights.

These behaviors begin to illustrate the irrevocable link that mobile and social have to how and what people buy—which is the real reason both are becoming so critical to marketers. So let's dive a bit more deeply into the role social channels can play in these interactions.

START WITH SOCIAL

Social media is the subset of digital related to social/sharing platforms such as Facebook, Twitter, YouTube, LinkedIn, Google+, Pinterest, Instagram, Tumblr, Snapchat, SlideShare, and Yik Yak, as well as numerous others too small to mention (or not yet invented). While digital marketing in general is about an interconnected world where information and content is easily accessed, social media platforms enable that information and other user-generated content to be more easily shared and discovered. Along with websites, Facebook and other social media platforms are key digital centers for gaining brand and program information, offering marketers more than just awareness and goodwill-building opportunities; they also provide opportunities for paid advertising, sophisticated targeting, and the ability to activate and amplify advocacy on behalf of brands.

A great demonstration of social media's power to reach unique targets by activating sharing and advocacy can be found in the US Navy's Project Architeuthis campaign. The effort was designed to recruit navy cryptologists, a notoriously difficult-to-fill role in its all-volunteer military force. Insights into this tiny and elusive group revealed that the most capable among them could not resist the lure of a challenging puzzle. Leveraging that insight, and with no paid media budget, the navy developed an augmented reality game (ARG) where all of the game's characters, information, puzzles, and coded clues were disseminated over eighteen days exclusively via social channels including Facebook, Twitter, Instagram, and Tumblr. Puzzles tasked players with cracking coded messages to enable the navy to disrupt an enemy plot. Fans of cryptology not only worked on the puzzles, but they also spread word of the game to other cryptologists, creating teams to help each other advance. The effort brought the navy to the attention of the cryptology community, and inspired them to not only self-identify, but also identify others with similar interests and skills, digitally linking the navy to all of the prospects. Thanks to the campaign, the US Navy met its recruiting goal ahead of schedule, and an analysis of the data revealed a high correlation between participation in the game, generated leads, and enlistment.[13]

An activation program for McDonald's also shows the power marketers have to link and amplify the voices of their brand advocates. To help celebrate the fortieth anniversary of Ronald McDonald House Charities and inspire millennials to become engaged supporters of it, McDonald's developed a hashtag—#forRMHC—so those who had benefited from the charity could share their stories in a more-connected way. While other touchpoints were employed, such as packaging and in-store materials, Facebook, Twitter, You-Tube, and Instagram formed the core of the program, and those alone, with the support of a few celebrity influencers, helped them generate more than twenty-four million impressions and raise $200 million.[14]

While the success of these campaigns is clear, marketers need to remember that in today's world, all media is essentially social media, and the goal of every marketer should be to drive sharing and word of mouth in everything they do, not just in their Facebook or social media strategy.

Experiential events, contests, giveaways, and even retail displays can all be opportunities to create content that can be shared, and, ideally, these activities should be designed with that purpose in mind. The power of experiential events, contests, and giveaways in particular is their inherent newsworthiness, which can inspire sharing, and in the process create valuable social proof for new prospects that demonstrates or reinforces a brand's promise and appeal. If a brand stands for the ability to help create and share happiness, for example, the marketer can go beyond simply claiming to create happiness in brand advertising, and instead do something that enables the target consumers to actually experience and share that happiness themselves.

This is precisely what Unilever did in Portugal when they created a vending machine for their ice-cream brands that did not accept money, but, rather, required smiles. Through facial recognition software, an individual was able to receive a free ice-cream product from the machine when he or she smiled—and then was able to share the happiness by uploading a picture of his or her smiling face to Facebook.[15] This created value for the participants, who were able to quickly and easily share the joy of their free sample and the unique experience that went with it, and for the marketer, who was able to deploy a sampling program without the usual expense of local street teams, and create positive word of mouth that built the brand by literally demonstrating its proposition.

So what types of content tend to get shared? According to Jonah Berger and Eric Schwartz in a working paper produced by the Marketing Science

Institute, people tend to talk about everyday items more than innovative breakthrough products[16]—which should be good news for most marketers. The opportunity for marketers is to give people a reason to talk about their brands and products—and help to enable it on social media. To fully empower this effort with real insight into what will motivate individual sharing and who will be most impacted by it, marketers need to utilize the principles and tools of the fourth component of the digital ecosystem—customer relationship management (CRM).

MANAGING THE RELATIONSHIP TO CRM

With digital's inherent link to CRM, direct, and database marketing, marketers have the ability to fully track and customize experiences, incent participation in ways that are truly meaningful to the recipient, drive sharing among their networks, and enable a transaction with a single click.

Of course, the ultimate goal of all of the above is to build long-term relationships with individuals that enable the marketer to garner greater insight into their wants and needs, and be better positioned to meet them with relevant and well-timed communications.

At the end of the day, mobile is a one-to-one medium, and as a result, the quantity and quality of information it can provide to marketers is formidable. Mining shared information, as well as the multiple sources of data generated through mobile usage, can yield insights leading to ultra-targeted programs that meet consumers' needs on a one-to-one basis. The CRM database and the primary data within it, as the backbone of it all, can enable marketers to understand an individual's path-to-purchase, as well as their needs along the way.

While this topic will be fully explored in chapter 7, the key concept to keep in mind is that every digital engagement is a data point that, when compiled, gives marketers the opportunity to use quantified behaviors to create custom audiences of consumers and shoppers who can receive the right information at the right time (right down to changing a website landing page based on the user's likely interests and needs), making any and all digital engagements targeted, customized, and potentially one-to-one.

The true power of the data is not just to understand with great precision what happened in the past, but also to accurately predict what will happen in the future, utilizing predictive models that enable marketers to anticipate needs and behaviors to create better experiences for their users—from optimal financial incentives, content, and sharing recommendations to more-effective loyalty programs.

This data is also the fuel that informs the algorithms for programmatic media buying (via automated systems), which is expanding to be employed by online messaging, video, dynamically generated creative content, and even broadcast television.[17] While much of the AIM can be employed without the use of programmatic media-buying technologies, its implementation can certainly be enhanced by programmatic efforts—just as programmatic efforts can be enhanced by the AIM.

Once a marketer understands the moments and the needs along the shopper's journey, content can be appropriately parsed to correspond to the needs at each point, changing how the marketer creates and delivers information. Lenovo, for example, went from developing long B2B product videos—each five to eight minutes in length—to producing shorter pieces that are "tailored to where the buyer is in the sales cycle." As a result of the shift, "video now ranks as Lenovo's No. 2 lead generator in terms of conversions to sales, right after e-books."[18]

BRINGING IT ALL TOGETHER

The marketers who successfully integrate digital, mobile, and social, with an understanding of how people shop and buy, and supported by data, have the underpinnings to deliver powerfully creative programs. Tesco in South Korea provides a great example.

South Koreans, among the hardest-working people in the world, dread going to grocery stores after their long work hours. So Tesco used this shopper insight to bring grocery shopping to them via virtual stores at subway stops. Images of products, arranged on shelves as they appear in stores, created an inviting user experience that instantly made people comfortable navigating the "aisles."

Shoppers could place products in virtual shopping carts by scanning QR codes with their smartphones. The products would then be delivered to their homes that evening, transforming static transit ads into retail transaction-driving opportunities. Sales soared, and excitement spread as people shared their experiences via social media. Participants received incentives to visit the Tesco website, and data was funneled into CRM programs to help shoppers stay happy and loyal. Online registrations and sales increased by 76% and 130%, respectively, and Tesco became the number-one online grocer and number-two grocer overall in South Korea.[19]

The Tesco case is just one example, but it highlights the opportunity to move mobile from the marketing periphery to the center by leveraging its unique opportunity to bring social, shopper, promotion, and CRM together to deliver creative, branded experiences people value. It also demonstrates how digital and experiential marketing can connect synergistically to unite the online and physical worlds.

Today's consumers, of course, do not live online or off-; they just live, moving fluidly across many if not all of the media channels. As Tesco so effectively demonstrates, brands need to do the same.

In fact, Elisa Montaguti, Scott Neslin, and Sara Valentini confirmed that "multichannel customers" are more profitable. It is not just that already-satisfied customers look for their favored brands across the on- and off-line worlds. It is actually just as much the opposite. They found that marketing efforts can drive currently single-channel customers to become multichannel, and, as a result, increase their satisfaction and profitability with a brand.[20]

OUT WITH THE OLD (CATEGORIES), IN WITH THE NEW

From a brand-activation perspective, the true power of digital and social media, particularly when mobile, falls into several categories that may represent a more-helpful way for marketers to organize the space and therefore more fully leverage its activation capabilities in any and all efforts going forward.

Individual technologies, platforms, and hardware will inevitably come, go, and evolve at an ever-accelerating pace, rendering any technology-specific recommendation potentially obsolete the moment it is given. However, when one considers the universe of digital capabilities from the perspective of their utility in activating human behaviors that move individuals closer to transaction, key opportunities emerge that provide a lens through which any individual technology, platform, or product can be evaluated and potentially utilized. These key opportunities include:

- *Connection*—the power to reach and connect with consumers/shoppers anywhere along their path-to-purchase and deliver relevant content ranging from invitations and incentives to instructions and video.
- *Conversation*—the power to enable a two-way exchange of information in real time that drives ongoing value for and engagement with individuals.

- *Optimization*—the power that digital data offers marketers to create optimal experiences for users by delivering the right content in the right way at the right time.
- *Amplification*—the power to amplify the voices of brand advocates to create new shoppers, consumers, and advocates.
- *Transaction*—the ability to transact instantly from anywhere.

This construct can help the marketer organize and assess options, particularly when aligned with insights into individual's unique paths-to-purchase, to make digital, social, and mobile marketing efforts more precisely focused on the key opportunities for behavior change that will increase the marketing program's overall effectiveness.

Starting with the power of *connection*, programmatic online advertising, contextual targeting (based on the interests of the user and the content of the environment), and paid and organic search engine marketing offer brands the opportunity to make sure targeted messages are available along key upper-funnel digital touchpoints to reach shoppers early on in their consideration process. E-mail marketing can offer the same benefits in reaching shoppers with whom brands have already established a relationship. Websites, Facebook pages, and YouTube channels can be central hubs for brand information and content, linked to all of the channels above, with, of course, mobile the conduit to all, utilizing location-aware opportunities to ensure that information is delivered to the right shopper at the right time.

Opportunities for *conversation* include developing and delivering programs individuals can participate in, versus simply messages they receive, ensuring ongoing engagement across more of the path-to-purchase. These programs can range from games and contests, to cause-related sponsorships and photo/video sharing, and all can potentially utilize even traditional media vehicles such as print, out of home (OOH), and brick-and-mortar retail displays via hashtags, text programs, visual recognition, or simple URLs. To drive any level of engagement, however, programs need to offer some form of value to the consumer—from the financial or experiential, to the functional or personal—in exchange for their participation and the valuable data it can provide.

The data provided across all touchpoints gives the marketers powerful tools of *optimization* that should be evident in thoughtfully designed user experiences across all environments, based on insights into how individuals utilize and access information. From dynamic landing pages to triggered e-mail messaging, marketers can segment their consumers/shoppers to make sure they are delivering the right types of information at the right time to their visitors. To take the next step toward true mass micro-personalization, every digital touchpoint should be treated as both an opportunity to opt in to future personalized communications, as well as a channel to deliver personalized financial incentives, content, and sharing recommendations to those who do. The latter group is enhanced by the ability to predictively model expected outcomes and action them via dynamic creative outputs.

Amplification is enabled via the strategic use of social media platforms, blogs, and photo/video sharing opportunities created via branded experiential events and often supported by paid media. Not all shares are created equal, leading marketers to identify opinion leaders or exceptionally connected consumers with whom to provide initial access to highly valued (and sharable) content or experiences.

Of course, all of the above is in service of driving consumers to *transaction*, which can now be as easily achieved by a mobile "buy now" button as it can be in-store. All digital interactions can and should enable the shopper to pull the trigger on the desired transaction at the moment he or she is ready, whether it is a purchase direct from the marketer or via a selected retail partner. Additionally, the ability to push financial incentives directly to a mobile wallet or passbook for future consideration, and then remind the shopper when they are in proximity of a retail channel for redemption, will become a more and more important aspect of marketing activation.

When aligned with each individual's unique, nonlinear path-to-purchase, digital, mobile, and social media arm the marketer with the opportunity to activate their brands by creating value for shoppers at each relevant touchpoint by leveraging digital's unique ability to drive connection, conversation, optimization, and amplification in service of the marketer's ultimate goal: transaction.

ONWARD

As is hopefully becoming clear, the real opportunity for the marketer is to look at digital as a unified ecosystem, accessed via mobile, socially enabled, with data-driven insights that can deliver the right content at the right time to the right individual. With that in mind, it is no wonder mobile advertising is booming, reaching $101.4 billion spent in 2016,[21] and continuing to increase.

But what is the role of content, and how can marketers optimize its relationship with context to enable them to fully maximize the ROI of their business- and brand-building efforts?

In the next chapter, we will explore content in its many forms, and the key role it can play in brand activation and the AIM.

6

Come and Get It

Content and In-Bound Marketing

As we have discussed, effective brand activation targets the key moments along the path-to-purchase where there are barriers to overcome or opportunities to accelerate movement toward transaction. Even when those key inflection points are identified, however, the marketer will not be successful in engaging the consumer, shopper, or prospect without creating sufficient value at or around those moments to motivate interaction.

While techniques from experiential and participation marketing can be powerfully applied, as we will explore in detail in chapter 8, sometimes the most effective and efficient way to deliver value in the moment is through a highly engaging piece of content.

Creating and distributing relevant and valuable content that fully engages a target audience is, of course, one of the foundational activities of marketing. Doing it both systematically and at scale, with a focus on content of inherent value independent of its relationship to the brand, is the specialized expertise of the content marketer, and it can be critical to advancing prospects along their shopper journeys.

According to the Content Marketing Institute, content marketing is defined as "the art of communicating with your customers and prospects without selling. It is non-interruption marketing. Instead of pitching your products or services, you (marketers) are delivering information that makes your buyer more intelligent."[1]

As they explain it, "[I]f we, as businesses, deliver consistent, ongoing valuable information to buyers, they ultimately reward us with their business and loyalty."[2]

There are, of course, a few critical steps in between.

BACK TO THE FUTURE

This marketing approach is certainly not new, as the Content Marketing Institute itself points out. Some historical examples they cite include *The Furrow* magazine, published by John Deere since 1895, with a focus on helping farmers improve their business skills; the world-renowned Michelin Guides; a recipe book from Jell-O; and the original soap operas launched by P&G in the 1930s. There are, of course, many other examples—from today's branded videos on YouTube to the 1960s book from International Paper that gave readers instructions on how to create different styles of paper airplanes to none-too-subtly drive additional usage of their products.[3]

Today, if marketers build better content, in the form of information or entertainment that customers find valuable, prospects will indeed come—powered by search engine optimization (SEO) and discovered through Google, Bing, or Yahoo; shared via their social channels; delivered directly through e-mail; or encountered through contextual online advertising or apps.

As Christine Crandell pointed out in a piece in *Customer Think*, "A significant portion of the early stages of the buyer's journey is driven by buyer self-discovery—from understanding the problem, alternative solution approaches, outcomes their peers have realized, and best practices."[4]

These are moments when relevant content can be powerfully appealing, particularly when easily accessible online. That is one of the reasons content marketing is one of the fastest-growing specialties in the industry,[5] and looks likely to continue to grow at least for the foreseeable future.[6]

But self-discovery and the exploration of new solutions and approaches can also happen deeper in the shopper's journey, or even after the point of transaction—often with greater complexity and more-specific needs—and as a result, appropriate content can be just as powerfully utilized. Marketers, therefore, should be conscious that content marketing has applications throughout the buyer (and user) journeys, and can be very effective at not just creating an on-ramp to a brand's consideration, but also at moving prospects further along the path at key points, keeping them from exiting via potential off-ramps, and even reassuring them post-purchase.

In content marketing efforts, the brand or marketer becomes the publisher and often owns or controls the environments where the content appears. Fortunately for today's brands and marketers, the publishing opportunities are virtually limitless.

A WORLD OF CHOICES

Content format and publishing options range from websites, apps, e-mail updates, newsletters (or e-newsletters), quizzes, webinars, podcasts, memes and blogs (or vlogs) to infographics, white papers (often called research or technical reports), slideshows, videos, e-books, printed books, checklists, guides, and even branded entertainment and product packaging. Anything that provides information or entertainment can be considered content.

From a brand-activation perspective, the form of content that is best for a specific brand or circumstance will depend on the image the brand aspires to convey about itself based on its essence and promise, the actions or behaviors it is hoping to inspire, and the needs, interests, and receptivity of its prospects at the point they will encounter the content. The form, therefore, needs to follow the function. For example:

- American Express wants to show their support for small businesses under the "Open" banner and inspire deeper involvement with its products, tools, and resources, so they curate the Open Forum, an online source for owners to gain business knowledge and networking opportunities.
- MAC Cosmetics wants to reinforce its history as the leading professional makeup authority that celebrates diversity and individuality, and spotlight its relevant products, so their e-commerce site features tutorials on how to create professional makeup effects that spotlight their makeup artists along with stories about diverse trendsetters.
- Anthropologie aims to project a hip, approachable lifestyle brand while they increase consumer time spent exposed to their products and offers, so they share interesting drink recipes on their blog.
- Callaway Golf wants to demonstrate that they are the brand that helps golfers improve their game, so they produce "how-to" videos featuring their products that they post on YouTube.

- Pampers aims to reach new parents and demonstrate that their brand is the key to raising happy, healthy babies, so they e-mail parenting tips to subscribers and post them online.

On the B2B side, players in the marketing technology field—such as Chango, Curata, HubSpot, Marketo, and others—are masters of the content marketing craft, teaching marketers how to more effectively apply digital, social, and content by practicing what they preach, all the while establishing themselves as thought leaders in these areas. (Of course, it is no coincidence that they sell the technology that they are teaching readers to employ.)

What connects these examples is that they are all helping the recipient solve a problem, fulfill a need, optimize experiences, or simply become better informed by providing content of value beyond the explicit utility or emotional benefit of their product or service. By educating, entertaining, or simply enlightening, all infused with subtle points of view, suggestions, and well-placed facts, the goal is to utilize content to engage prospects while putting the pieces in place that will ultimately help them to discover that he or she needs or wants the sponsoring brand's product. Done well, particularly in a B2B environment, the content can even help the drive toward consensus among key stakeholders that is required in group decisions, as the information shared can help frame discussions and bring focus to the issues, options, and decision-making criteria.

IF YOU WANT ANSWERS, FIRST ASK QUESTIONS

To help determine the best topics, tone, and form of the content that will drive brand activation, marketers need to begin by asking some critical qualifying questions, including:

1. What do my shoppers or prospects want or need to know, and when do they want or need to know it? Getting the right content into the right place so that it is easily discoverable or accessible at the right time with the right amount of depth is key to activating purchase behaviors.
2. When and where will the content be obtained and viewed, and if online, from what kind of device? The optimal form may be different if it is likely being viewed from a desktop in an office rather than on a smartphone in a noisy big box retailer.

3. If the content is to be discovered during an online search, what are the likely triggers that will inspire the search? If the content is about ease of use, for example, the tone and form of the delivery will need to be different if it is designed for someone considering a purchase versus someone having trouble using the product.

4. Who will be viewing the content? Marketers, of course, will want to match the content as closely as possible with the interests and preferences of the recipient. On a macro level, those interests can vary by demographics and psychographics[7]—baby boomers, for example, interestingly "have the highest preference for articles under 200 words" as well as "strong preference for articles over 500 words" when compared against Gen-X and Millennial audiences[8]—as well as based on the individual's unique circumstances, motivations, and needs.[9]

5. Where is the recipient on his or her shopper journey? Since the motivations, interests, needs, pain points, and opportunities change and evolve along the path, so, too, should the content. What is relevant at one point on the path may not be at another, so content cannot always be repurposed. Rather, it may need to be rethought in order to provide the relevant and valuable information at each point.

6. Finally, what is the behavior the marketer is trying to inspire? Is it to drive an inquiry so the prospect takes the first step in their shopper journey? Is it to drive sharing, so the prospect can bolster their social currency while spreading the word for the marketer's brand? Or is it to encourage the consumer to try utilizing a product in a new way, so the brand becomes more integral to the consumer's life? The answer is important, because the form can help to drive the behavior just as much as the content can, so the desired behavior should play a role in the strategy for both.

One popular strategy to help manage the questions and decisions above is for marketers to create buyer personas—with inputs drawn from customer interactions, posts on select social media sites, and insights from sales teams—to help the content creators determine the best approach and tone. This method can enable marketers to better focus their efforts against a detailed picture of the ultimate recipient, so the individual becomes more real for all involved. It can, however, be limiting or even damaging to content creation efforts if the data is drawn from too small of a pool; is based disproportionally on the hopes, aspirations, or biases of key stakeholders (such as the CEO, CMO, marketing director, or sales teams); or is driven by desires to push a specific product or solution rather than actually identifying the needs of the user or viewer.

A more-effective approach is to leverage data representing actual prospect and purchaser behavior, comparing clicks and downloads by specific individuals in similar situations, as well as examining the types of queries they make and searches they conduct along their shopper journeys. While qualitative insights for tonality may be drawn from an audit of posts on social media, the core inputs should be drawn from a wider audience than is typically found in user persona construction, and the result needs to align with the tonality of the brand. Kmart, for example, looked at the style of writing on their customers' Facebook posts to justify the humor and innuendo in their Effie Award–winning "Ship My Pants" campaign—but this was done in the aggregate, and in comparison with the tonality of their competition.[10]

CONTENT RICH

Content can be utilized to create the initial engagement with consumers/shoppers that ultimately connects them to the digital ecosystem that will manage all engagements going forward, or it can be the way that those ongoing communications are managed once the target opts in. In many cases, it may be both.

As a result, a content strategy for each shopper segment needs to be developed that aligns content opportunities with all of the key touchpoints along the path-to-purchase where there may be potential off-ramps or speed bumps, or where there are opportunities to accelerate movement toward transaction.

Once the right target has been identified, along with the right points to reach him or her along the shopper journey, and in the right ways, the challenge becomes how to maximize the value of the content offered to the individual to most effectively drive engagement.

At the highest level, marketers can begin to consider potential types of content as falling into one of several categories:

- Content the target is already interested in, borrowing interest from their existing passion points, such as music, sports, movies, or fashion, but curated or created by the brand. This is typically an easy place to start, as everyone has interests, but can be challenging to execute in a differentiated and brand-ownable way.

- Content that will self-select a target audience, such as articles on baby-proofing a home that will likely only be of interest to new or soon-to-be new parents and grandparents. This type of content can be particularly effective in generating hand-raisers who self-identify as targets early in their shopping journey when initial targeting information may be limited.
- Content that will explicitly target shoppers currently in the category, such as articles about how to manage a renovation more effectively from a home improvement retailer. This is an obvious place to start, but needs to be carefully managed to overcome potential perceptions of bias to deliver credible utility.
- Content designed to reach a target actively considering your brand, such as a chef's series on food pairings with beers based on taste profiles from a craft brewer, or a guide to safe driving from a car company trying to show its unrelenting focus on safety. These types of content can be very effective in driving cross-sell or upsell among current buyers or in closing the sale with new ones.
- Content that a target already engaged with your brand will be interested in, either to share with other prospects or to build their engagement and loyalty, such as tips to get the most out of a phone's camera function from a professional photographer.

Thanks to the power of data, and the ability to predictively model expected outcomes, marketers can increase the precision with which they align content with individuals. This alignment can happen at an aggregate level, where individuals are sorted into a finite number of segments, each with a different set of associated content, or at an individual level, where individual interests and behaviors trigger customized and personalized responses.

Using the passion-point example above, an aggregate-level approach might determine who gets music content, who gets sports content, and who receives fashion content, or at a greater level of precision, who gets country-and-western content, who gets hip-hop, and who gets heavy metal. These types of interactions are typically managed by a static set of business rules that are applied based on a defined set of parameters.

This approach can be taken to a greater level of sophistication, however, by utilizing dynamic, self-learning models that calibrate responses against results to optimize individualized content matching in real time. The goal can be not just to deliver the right piece of content to the right person at the right time, but also to begin to serve up content going forward that represents the "next best action"—a concept from CRM and database marketing—to most efficiently continue the target on the path toward transaction. In the case of one prospect, an initial targeted piece of content may be best followed by a third-party review, whereas for another individual, it may best be followed by a link to more curated content related to a target passion point.

By monitoring who engages with what, when, and how, the models can begin to calibrate what is served to whom, and when, in order to best increase engagement, and, ultimately, transactions.

A typical best practice in developing these models is the "champion/challenger" approach, where the current model runs as the champion, but a challenger model runs continuously in the background, trying to outperform the champion. When it does, it is moved into the champion role, only to do battle with future challenger models in an ongoing effort to optimize the model's predictive power.

Regardless of the approach to determine the next best action, the larger point is to both optimize the relationship between prospect and content, and to consider content as part of an overall communications ecosystem that can move a prospect, for instance, from casual engagement to opting in for future contact, to telegraphing interests, to sharing with other prospects, and ultimately to purchasing. Realizing this kind of approach will require a clearly defined content strategy, editorial processes, governance, workflow processes, content management, production, and measurement protocols calibrated against behavioral objectives. All of the above will also need to be carefully managed to ensure that all communications are consistent with the voice and tone of the brand, or at least complementary to the brand in the case of borrowed interest content.

While one can certainly say that all marketing is content marketing, because all marketing has "content" (just as one can say all marketing is shopper marketing or experiential marketing, because all marketing is trying to influence shoppers, and creates experiences), it is important to identify and leverage the unique expertise of each of these specialties. The unique and leverageable expertise of the content marketer lies in managing the complexities of content strategy, editorial process, workflow process, and governance, and the ability to efficiently develop and systematize content across multiple publishers and platforms.

As segments and touchpoints increase, including toward a true mass micro-personalization approach, it becomes increasingly complex to ensure that every piece of content is consistent with the content strategy and brand, that it is legally vetted, produced in all of the required forms and formats, and cataloged and tagged for both internal and external access. As a result, it is critical to establish a process to manage content in all of its various forms.

One of the oft-repeated rules of thumb in content marketing is COPE: Create Once, Publish Everywhere. While clearly a bit of an overstatement—given that marketers want to be strategic with what they publish, where, and that each channel will require creation according to its own parameters—the idea is to try to think systemically to identify content-creation efficiencies where a single piece of content can be strategically repurposed and reformatted to produce maximum value. A white paper's content, for example, once authored, can also be visualized via video, delivered in a live-streaming presentation, or selectively excerpted to create infographics and other types of short-form web content. The key is to take a cross-channel mind-set from the beginning of the content-creation process, looking to develop content with maximum adaptability and scalability across media.

Marketers need to be careful, however, to ensure that all of the content is appropriate for the channel and, especially, for the prospects' mind-set when the content is accessed. In other words, they need to guarantee that they are not just blindly filling up content channels. Occasionally content practitioners can get so caught up in "feeding the machine" by producing new content pieces (or repurposing existing ones just to fill channels) that they may overlook the goal of moving prospects along the path-to-purchase and focus too heavily on one need state (such as awareness) while missing other key roadblocks (such as usage occasions).

On the flip side, it is also important to approach all marketing efforts with an eye toward potential content-creation opportunities, whether it is simply capturing video of a brand event or interviewing key partners or stakeholders. In developing sponsorship relationships, for example, there are often many content-creation opportunities that can be taken advantage of if identified and planned for from the outset. For example, a tie-in with a film or television property can often include access to new or existing interviews with directors, producers, special effects experts, or stars, all of which can be utilized as short- or long-form text or video content. These opportunities are often underutilized artifacts of existing sponsorships, or can be easily negotiated up front with an eye toward future content marketing needs.

THE BENEFITS OF OWNERSHIP

With a clearly defined brand idea and marketing calendar, the marketer's strategic and creative leadership can begin to identify and create content that is truly consistent with the brand idea and marketing plans, but tailored to specific segments and occasions. While content will be customized and served up strategically to different targets at different points in time, it is critical to make sure that from the perspective of each individual, all of the brand's communications add up to a cohesive, branded whole. This is where tightly calibrated cascading creative briefs become key.

From a clearly defined brand, an overarching marketing idea can be briefed and developed to bring the brand to life in a relevant way during a specific period of time. That marketing idea, once determined, then needs to be translated into all of the relevant touchpoints that align with the path-to-purchase of the highest-value consumer or shopper target, as well as the other priority segments. Each of those touchpoints represent the next set of creative briefs. Content can then be created for each brief that will drive engagement at those key inflection points, in a way that is consistent with not only the overarching brand idea, but also the marketing idea for that period of time.

For example, Coca-Cola's brand idea may be "Open Happiness," and its marketing idea during the holidays may be a cause-related program called "Arctic Home," in which every purchase of Coca-Cola goes to save the habitat of the real-world equivalent of their holiday icons, the polar bears. When a web film chronicling the reduction in habitat for the polar bears is distributed online and promoted via cinema spots, that content is consistent with both the Arctic Home holiday idea and the overarching brand idea of the joy that can be created by simply opening a Coke. Additionally, the content aligns with the shoppers' path-to-purchase by creating awareness of the opportunity to do good at the point of purchase, and inviting the shopper to opt in to participate and learn more. When a consumer opts in and begins receiving targeted communications tied to the appropriate retail partner, that content not only aligns with the shoppers' path-to-purchase, but it also ladders up to the larger program brand and marketing idea, as well.

The requirements of creating all the types of content that a marketer may choose to utilize may increase the need for new types of content creators, moving beyond traditional creative teams to include journalists, filmmakers, scriptwriters, authors, and others. With a clearly defined brand and marketing idea, a tightly constructed cascading series of briefs, and the oversight of strategic and creative leadership, however, effective content can be developed that is on brand, on strategy, and efficiently repurposed across appropriate platforms regardless of its form or source.

THE RIGHT CONTENT AT THE RIGHT TIME

As we have discussed, content can be a key tool in taking advantage of the shopper-based insights into the path-to-purchase and the abilities of digital channels to deliver timely engagement when and where needed. What is also clear is that utilizing the tools of direct/database marketing and CRM, today's marketers have the opportunity to maximize efficiency and effectiveness by delivering content that has maximum value to each recipient at each point along their unique path toward transaction.

A deeper dive into the activation power of those disciplines is the subject of our next chapter.

7

The Importance of Being Direct (Database and CRM, Too)

Activating a brand means stimulating behaviors in the brand's target consumers, shoppers, or prospects that help move them toward the marketer's ultimate goal—transaction. Consequently, marketers must know where the targets are in their shopping process; the paths they typically take; what offers, experiences, information, or other content would most interest them; and how that content or incentive is best delivered—all based on how those targets have responded in the past, in order to best anticipate, calibrate, and react to future responses.

While this certainly sounds like a tall order, marketers are more and more able to deliver on these requirements thanks to ever-increasing data sources, capabilities, and tools that can be utilized in conjunction with the proven approaches and best practices from the fields of direct, database, and customer relationship marketing. In a data-rich world, these specialties are marketers' new best friends, helping to identify the key behavioral points for each shopper and deliver the right message to the right individual at the right time, making them critical to realizing the full potential of the AIM.

What is more, direct, database, and CRM expertise (for our discussion, we will refer to them collectively as "direct") can also help marketers develop key insights into consumers' new, multiple, nonlinear paths-to-purchase, enabling them to customize communications based on what, where, how, and when to best engage their prospects, as well as on prospects' responses to each interaction, enabling marketers to optimize their messaging going forward.

As every modern marketer is acutely aware, the ubiquity of cross-linked digital media is enabling data capture on a massive scale. To emphasize the point, eMarketer reports that the average person in the UK has more than 3,000 pieces of personal information stored about him or her every week, from details about web, social, and mobile phone use to shopping behaviors, banking habits, loyalty program usage, and even their locations throughout the day.[1] This flood of incoming digital data will only continue to build. Mobile marketing spending, to pick one data-rich channel as an example, is expected to increase 32% to $1.34 billion by 2017, according to ABI Research.[2]

Traditionally, however, utilizing the predictive power of data was the exclusive realm of direct response mediums, such as direct mail, e-mail, and customer loyalty programs, and they typically required a relationship with the consumer to build the original data sets. But now marketers can leverage digital channels to gain key insights, and virtually all digital marketing communications can be treated like direct response vehicles.

As all media become addressable, all marketing communications are becoming one-to-one, and the often-ignored practices of direct, particularly within business-to-consumer (B2C), are moving to the center of virtually every marketing effort.

While data has always played a role in the most sophisticated marketing efforts, it has traditionally been through the rearview measurement of past behaviors, such as the response rates of direct marketing, self-reported qualitative assessments, or activities marketers siloed as CRM. In contrast, predictive analytics, using the increasingly available digital data, is forward-looking. It enables marketers to model data to anticipate what is likely to happen if an individual receives a certain message, invitation, or incentive as part of a creative communication at a designated point in their engagement.

In the very near future, all marketers will be working toward creating perfectly designed, human-centered experiences individualized to what they know about each person and delivering only the offers and content that are most relevant and appropriate for that individual. This mass micro-personalization will enable every interaction with a brand to be truly tailored to the individual's likes, dislikes, past purchases, and current needs, as well as other relevant criteria, including their potential value to the marketer.

Even today, the predictive power of available data can enable marketers to know which shoppers are worth targeting, how valuable they are, how much should be invested, how to drive more purchases and/or greater loyalty, and who in their social graph the marketer would most want the prospect to share content with to drive future transactions. If even the smallest incremental improvements are made in these critical decisions, marketing dollars and efforts are more precisely focused where they will generate greater value, and as a result, the improvements in return on marketing investment can be substantial.

As Patrick Palmer, strategy and analytics lead at VSA Partners, puts it, "This is one way that marketers can apply maximum leverage with finite investments. Just as Paul DePodesta helped Billy Beane find the optimal investment in baseball players on a limited salary cap by focusing on on-base percentage, as chronicled in the book and film *Moneyball*, marketers can focus tightly on the prospective customers and metrics that truly matter in driving the business. Think of it as 'moneyball marketing.' "[3]

This capability is even extending to what had previously been considered traditional media channels, including television. Advances in addressable television advertisements, made possible via set-top boxes, shine a light on a world where even broadcast TV begins to behave in a one-to-one manner. An addressable TV ad campaign for Honda's Acura TLX luxury sedan combined anonymized sales data and other data-mining technology to choose 1.7 million households to show Acura ads. Those households' rate of buying the cars was more than 60% higher than that of a demographically similar control group who were not shown the ads.[4] As explored in chapter 3, we are reaching the point where two households living next to each other and watching the same program at the same time can and will receive different broadcast advertising, such as dog food ads for the dog owners and cat food ads for the cat owners.

While some companies continue down the traditional road of mass advertising, more and more are taking advantage of the growing opportunity to better understand, reach, and engage their brands' potential consumers and advocates in a more-personalized way. For them, the result has been a sea change in how their creative products are conceived, implemented, and measured—from online advertising, websites, and mobile applications to broadcast spots, print ads, events, and even outdoor.

BEST PRACTICES START HERE

Creativity and data science may not seem like the most intuitive bedfellows, but better bridging their two domains is one of the key shifts required to better drive brand activation in today's interconnected world. One can understand these changes by considering four specific opportunities for the creative development process and data science to intersect:

1. *Predictively inform the creative direction.*

    The rise of the strategic planning discipline has been, in part, a result of its ability to synthesize insights that inspire great work by creative teams. Predictive analytics, properly applied, has the potential to increase their abilities and take their insights and inspiration to the next level. In the right hands, predictive models can provide guidance, guidelines, or even boundaries for creative teams based on data-fueled insights into what types of messages, programs, or offers are likely to produce the desired results from key consumers.

    Great creative thinkers typically value actionable insights that can provide them a springboard to truly unique and effective solutions. This will still be the case, regardless of the origin of those insights. Despite the concerns by traditionalists that predictive algorithms will replace human creativity, these insights should not, could not, and will not replace creative inspiration, but instead, when properly utilized, can be powerful catalysts for it.

    At this point in the process, the data scientists and their predictive models can function in service of informing and inspiring creative teams to deliver the most engaging creative work possible.

2. *Create data-sharing opportunities.*

    As more and more creative communications take a digital form, marketers realize more and more possibilities to organically build the data-collection opportunities into them. From an online ad unit to a mobile app, there are myriad places where the seamless integration of data-sharing occasions can create value for both the consumer and the marketer, as well as enhance (or at least not interfere with) the consumer's experience.

    The marketing challenge is to conceive these opportunities so they deliver what each consumer values and to build them into experiences in authentic and organic ways. Both of these goals are best achieved when opportunities are designed into interactions from the outset.

    This is another place where collaborations between data scientists and their creative cohorts can be so powerful and effective. By identifying what marketers are hoping to learn about their consumers to more effectively serve them, tailoring the engagements to create value for them, and planning for the seamless integration of data-capture opportunities, brands can take a large step toward delivering the right message to the right audience at the right time.

If the marketer's goal is to continue and deepen engagement with their consumers, creatively learning about and authentically providing what the consumer values will always be a powerful tool. It will also inform the creation of future content and experiences that will drive opt-in, engagement, and sharing. After all, the only reliable way to deliver a consumer or shopper something of value, a foundational principle of the AIM, is to know what that individual finds valuable.

3. *Target creative executions.*

Predictive models can become the basis upon which targeted creative executions are conceived, designed, developed, and deployed. As more marketing becomes one-to-one, the ability to model individuals' expected responses to programs, offers, and messages can make developing targeted creative elements more efficient and executing them more effective.

Data scientists can provide their creative coworkers with valuable insights into the types of communications that will generate the desired results, as well as invaluable cautions as to potential unintended consequences highlighted by their models.

These collaborations can provide guidance to not only the content of the creative product, but also to its form, including the optimal media channel for delivery. In other words, as the marketing communications become more individualized, the resulting creative product will not only provide consumers with the experiences they will find more valuable, but they will also drive more-frequent interactions between creative teams and their data science counterparts.

In addition, these predictive models are what inform the creation of dynamic, built-on-the-fly advertising messages, which we explored in chapter 3, assembling all of the visual and verbal elements based on context and target. This form of creative development requires the creation of layout templates and related messaging elements—both images and text—that can be combined in myriad ways based on the audiences and/or contexts defined by the marketer, from location, time of day, and weather, to competitive actions, search history, likes, and purchases.

4. *Optimize creativity predictively.*

Optimizing messaging had traditionally taken the form of in-market testing, A/B testing, comparing two versions' performance, or qualitative evaluations. With predictive analytics, however, the expected responses to creative elements can be modeled before they appear in-market, creating opportunities to optimize their execution and pre-calibrate the in-market expectations. Modeling the expected impact of creative elements creates a fourth opportunity for the intersection of creativity and data science.

Once again, the data scientist can provide a valuable service to creative teams, enabling them to preview how the consumer would respond to creative elements and test any adjustments they would like to make. This interaction can enable the creative teams to explore which of a series of potential campaigns, messages, or calls-to-action they are considering is predicted to be most engaging to their consumer. The model can become a creative tool that facilitates exploration, validates instincts, and identifies pitfalls, long before any piece of creative makes it to market.

WELCOME TO THE DIRECT ECOSYSTEM

As we have discussed as one of the foundational aspects of the AIM, the currently fragmented marketing disciplines should no longer be thought of separately, but instead as key components of an interconnected ecosystem, in much the same way that the neurological, respiratory, and digestive systems are specialized with unique requirements and capabilities, but work together synergistically to power a healthy human body.

To extend this analogy to the world of direct and its potential to deliver mass micro-personalization, we can think of the marketer's data sources as

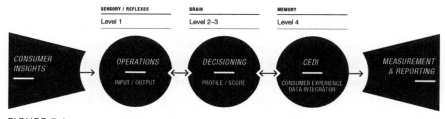

FIGURE 7.1
The foundations of a mass micro-personalization ecosystem.
Source: VSA Partners.

the "memory," the decisioning models that determine the next best action (be they targeted content, incentives, or invitations) as the "brain," and the direct channels themselves (largely digital) as both the "reflexes" that deliver the corresponding actions in the world and the "senses" that capture responses in the world and feed the data to the "memory" so it can be used to calibrate the "brain's" next decisions. Programmatic media buying can be considered the "arms and legs" that bring the marketing actions to the target prospects.

One of the most powerful direct channels, as we have discussed, is mobile, because each device is uniquely identifiable and virtually always with the individual. The uniquely tailored communications delivered through mobile by the marketer could simply be to align the shopper with the right retailer based on their proximity or basic demographic information, or it can be as sophisticated as delivering predictively modeled financial or experiential incentives weighted to the individual's immediate or long-term value to the brand. In either case, utilizing the principles and personalization of the direct ecosystem creates the opportunity to bring a true consumer focus to marketing efforts by giving brands the opportunity to identify individual paths-to-purchase; the location of critical barriers and opportunities along them; and the optimal content, experiences, and incentives to address them. Of course, as mobile adoption and usage continues to increase, the capabilities of marketers to focus and personalize their communications will also increase.

The development of this ecosystem, however, is leading some traditional marketers to raise the objection that predictive analytics, programmatic buying, and behaviorally driven messaging cuts emotionality out of the creative solution, when, in fact, they can make emotionality more targeted.

Programmatically created and behaviorally driven messaging certainly does lend itself to the delivery of rational propositions. Any contextual communication absolutely has to be clear and to the point, with a relevant and understandable call-to-action, to be effective. One will see this on display in most direct response vehicles, from snail mail to online, via the clear structure of the offer and call-to-action. The reason is that people need to know what to do in order to do it.

Of course, it has always been a much simpler challenge to create rational marketing communications than emotive ones, regardless of channel. As marketing strategist and psychologist Adam Ferrier puts it in his book, *The Advertising Effect: How to Change Behavior*, "It's much easier to generate and communicate a killer fact about a brand than it is to build emotion into the brand through advertising."[5]

However, Ferrier also points out that "the brain is able to process emotions without cognitions," so they get processed faster and with less effort than rational thoughts, adding that "our brain is more attracted to powerful emotional stimuli."[6] The effect is that consumers are more likely to remember and respond to emotional messages. Therefore, the goal and opportunity for the direct ecosystem is to do both in the proper balance, and in a uniquely tailored and targeted way to maximize messaging impact and in-market results.

THE NEED TO GET EMOTIONAL

It is the role of the creative teams—informed by strategies based on data and the insights they provide—to make the resulting creative messaging as effective as possible, which means utilizing the emotionality and rationality in appropriate combination. It was true back in the Mad Men era, and it is true today. Now we simply have an increased ability to deliver the right creative combination to the right person at the right moment.

Direct marketing has always produced numerous examples of effective communications that convey warmth, humor, fun, joy, or other emotions, in addition to its rational messaging. Just consider the ALS Association's "Ice Bucket Challenge," which delivered a clear call to action via digital or social channels directly to the individual challenged, but was laden with both emotions for the cause and humor at the act of dumping a bucket of ice over one's head.

While the soft-sell versus hard-sell debate goes back more than a hundred years,[7] today's discussions and concerns about the rationality-emotionality continuum simply point to the evolving skill set requirements for today's creative teams within a digital and data-enabled environment—a transformation that has not yet been fully realized.

First, as was pointed out by Debra Aho Williamson in the webinar "Creating Ads on the Fly—New Opportunities in Programmatic," creative teams will need to move away from solely developing highly polished communication pieces to instead developing a vision for a highly polished whole that will be created dynamically out of the elemental pieces, optimized to look seamless when assembled, but with so many potential variations that the team could not create all of them individually.[8] Since one of the most motivating

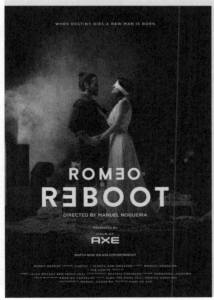
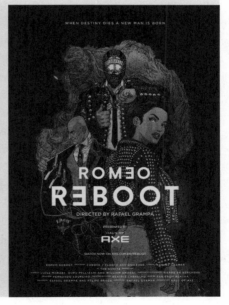

FIGURE 7.2
Unilever's Axe in Brazil created 100,000 different versions of a faux movie trailer based on target consumers' musical, brand, and consumption preferences.
Source: Romeo Reboot, created by CUBOCC/FLAGCX and UNILEVER.

aspects of the creative craft is to ultimately be able to hold and admire a finished piece, this new creative developmental process will require a notable shift in mind-set, increased creative conceptual abilities, and highly evolved production capabilities and processes.

Second, agency worlds need to collide in new, different, and inspiring ways. The new world of marketing—and effectively implementing the AIM— will require a new kind of creative practitioner.

In traditional agencies, marketers find that creatives and analysts live in different worlds, likely never working together, or even meeting. In today's leading-edge firms, a diverse group of cross-disciplinary creatives and data scientists not only sit side by side, but also collaborate, finding new ways to hardwire opportunities for data capture and utilization throughout the creative campaigns. These partnerships will help foster a new breed of creative thinker, one who is imagining new ways to add value to the consumer experience by adding value to the brand experience (and even to the product or service itself), new opportunities to deepen stories, and innovative ways to tailor content to individuals—creatively utilizing the insights and opportunities spotlighted by their data science partners.

The growing influx of data-driven insights is by necessity moving beyond the realm of researchers and planners to where it can be utilized to greatest advantage—in the development and execution of creative communications. What used to be considered the back end of creative development is now up front, and rather than constricting creativity, it can actually open doors to new, varied creative ideas that are measurably more effective in producing business results and affinity with a brand. That is the real potential power when data science and creativity meet.

More and more, today's top creative talent will need to bring the left and right brain together to produce inspired and measurably effective cross-channel marketing programs. One can think of this new evolution as an "analytic creative"—someone comfortable with utilizing the insights, opportunities, and variations identified by their data science and strategic planning partners, yet just as creative in their ability to develop and design breakthrough ideas and messaging as the "Mad Men" who preceded them—if not more so.

This should come as no surprise. The ability to develop inspired, right-brain solutions within a strategic framework of actionable intelligence is the creative currency of a data-driven age, and the real power of today's creatives.

Just as the rise of the strategic planning function within the agency world created a new partner and new set of inputs for today's creative teams, the best firms are already incorporating data-driven insights and opportunities—and the best creatives are once again rising to the occasion.

Consider Unilever's program for Axe out of Brazil, which created 100,000 different versions of a faux movie trailer for a supposed Shakespeare remake, *Romeo Reboot*. Based on target consumers' musical, brand, and consumption preferences, Axe developed four consumer segments, each of which was offered 25,000 permutations of the video, for 100,000 in all. Axe validated the segments via testing that monitored completed viewings and other feedback, and they continued to optimize the creative based on results in market.[9]

That final point is an important one. The days of "set it and forget it" are long gone. With real-time data come real-time opportunities to learn and improve messaging, offers, and results. This is a key learning from the world of direct marketing that has more and more applicability to a growing group of communication channels—and is a key aspect of the AIM. When a marketer is focused on activating behaviors, their world is inherently measurable—and whatever can be measured can be optimized.

The opportunity for advantage could not be greater: creating programs with pinpoint accuracy that optimize brand engagement by delivering the right message to the right person at the right moment to create more value for consumers and brands.

Bridging the chasm, of course, requires engineering on several sides: data scientists who understand the needs of creatives, strategic planners who can distill and communicate actionable inputs for creative teams, and creatives who can understand the implications of data-derived insights and can act on them. It is an issue and opportunity many are wrestling with, and many are making substantial progress.

Clearly, this is just scratching the surface of the real opportunity to unlock the power of the analytic creative.

As data-driven insights continue to change the world of marketing, the identification and cultivation of creative talent will need to change with it. The sources of talent will need to broaden as the expectations continue to grow, and the development of those identified reinvented and reprioritized. The opportunity, however, will more than reward the effort, as brands begin to enjoy more-engaging and -effective marketing efforts, and consumers enjoy participating in programs carefully designed to meet their needs, fit their interests, and deliver more valued brand experiences.

It won't be long before the industry may finally put to rest the age-old stereotype of the creative as a right-brained prima donna oblivious to the realities of clients' businesses. Of course, this new creative evolution will not be fully realized until marketers demand it.

SOLUTIONS, SOLUTIONS, SOLUTIONS

As we have already seen in our discussions of brand advertising, shopper, content, and direct, the new digital landscape—informed by data—is not only changing the ability to deliver relevant messaging, but also the ability to deliver it at appropriate points in the shopper's journey.

One of the keys to the AIM is to look for digitally enabled opportunities to treat every channel as a direct channel, aligned with the barriers and opportunities along each consumer or shopper's unique, nonlinear path-to-purchase. The goal is to deliver what is truly the next best action—be it information, invitation, incentive or validation—based on insights into the individual, to create maximum value for both the consumer and the marketer. For example, the next best action at the moments prior to transaction for a shopper identified as "price sensitive" might be to share social content praising the value of the product along with a time-sensitive gift with purchase offer. For a "status seeker," the next best action may be to share red carpet video of a celebrity wearing the product along with an invitation to an exclusive event.

The opportunity is tremendous: to create an optimal consumer experience, built on the unique intersections between the brand and the needs and wants of the individual, that results in increased affinity, loyalty, and advocacy—and an optimal marketing effort that maximizes ROI by building the brand as well as the business.

Now join us as we look at one of the main engagement drivers behind the AIM—the invitations, offers, experiences, and incentives that are designed to drive participation.

Insights into individuals and their unique paths-to-purchase can only be fully activated by creating sufficient value to drive engagement. In the next chapter, we will discuss the tools, techniques, and unique strengths of promotion and participation marketing, a discipline that had traditionally been viewed as residing firmly on the business-building side of the marketing equation, but is now recognized for its power in brand building as well.

8

Join Us

The World of Participation and Promotion Marketing

It is no secret that under a variety of labels and guises, participation and promotion marketing have moved to the center of companies' marketing efforts. These methods are becoming increasingly important as brands intensify their focus on incenting consumers to opt in and encouraging the behaviors that move prospects closer to the brand and a transaction.

It is also widely understood that these efforts can play an invaluable role in activating behaviors among key constituents, such as the sales force, associates, distributors, retailers, and other company stakeholders who are critical to engaging the brand's consumers.

But what some may not be aware of is the full extent to which these key practices can be and are being employed across other marketing disciplines. A broad range of traditional participation and promotion tactics—such as games, contests, discounts, sampling, sweepstakes, premiums, and many more—are rapidly being reinvented for the digital age and enabling marketers to drive engagement, inspire sharing, and propel transactions like never before. Couponing, for example, is so pervasive online that it is virtually enabling targeted pricing. Games and gaming constructs are being used with greater frequency in apps and on the web to engage consumers and teach them about brands and their values, features, and benefits. Social media platforms are now some of the key channels for communicating limited-time discounts, incentives, and other participation opportunities.

Beyond their digital applications, promotion and participation marketing strategies and tactics have become so mainstream—and so effective—that they are now pervasive across all marketing channels and efforts, from the Pepsi Challenge, Coca-Cola's Arctic Home, and McDonald's Monopoly games, to seventy-two-hour test drives, pop-up retail events, and flash sales. Additionally, internal or system motivation programs that have traditionally relied largely on the use of incentives are now including the fun, experiential adventures of games and other consumer-style tactics. Of course, trade and channel sales-building programs have long used promotions as the "push" side complement to the consumer "pull" efforts, and are often where the largest portion of the marketing budget is allocated for B2C companies. Increasingly, however, even within the world of B2B, sales contests and other behavior-driving programs are also taking on the sophisticated sheen of mainstream consumer promotions.

Now, with the ability to individualize messaging and offers, virtually every invitation to participate can be experienced as highly relevant and highly valuable to each shopper or prospect, creating an interaction that is not only unique to the brand, but also appropriate to the individual as well.

The result are programs that are not just communicating the brand's essence, promise, and key features and benefits, but also demonstrating them, all while incenting the very behaviors that move a shopper closer to transaction, an employee closer to aligning his or her work performance with the goals of a company initiative, or a sales representative closer to achieving specific sales results.

Indeed, whenever a marketer has a behavioral objective, the engagement-based techniques of promotion and participation marketing can play a role in demonstration, education, and motivation. Even when a brand fulfills its promise, the resulting satisfied consumers can be encouraged with these techniques to share their experiences and love of the brand with others via social media, providing future consumers with the testimonials they may need when researching brands or seeking validation post-purchase. With these types of tactics, consumers can also be incented to opt in to receive future brand communications, which may include additional targeted offers, content, or opportunities to engage.

While long considered largely focused on the business-building side of the marketing equation, participation and promotion marketing are now fully understood to be key components of driving the types of engagement that are critical to marketers' brand-building efforts as well.

Of course, the most sophisticated practitioners have long taken advantage of their abilities to build both brand and business. Just consider Coca-Cola's limited-edition Sundblom Santa holiday packaging and resulting association with the holiday imagery that goes back to 1931; Cracker Jack's famous prize inside; General Mills' beloved Box Tops for Education; or Wheaties' limited-edition packaging that literally demonstrates its positioning as "the Breakfast of Champions," and one can see how integral these types of programs have historically been in building brands as well as driving business.

One of the great examples of perennially doing both is Kellogg's "Special K Challenge." At its foundation, it is a promotional tactic that drives two weeks of increased product usage, and yet it also communicates a key brand benefit—facilitating weight loss and maintenance—to such a degree that the challenge has become a key branding tool for not only the cereal, but also all of its related products.

In many instance, the distinction between the program and the marketer's brand becomes indiscernible, such as with McDonald's Happy Meal. Is it a brand or a promotion? It is a regular menu item that conveys a branded promise of fun and parent-child bonding, but the actual offer changes each month and drives multiple visits to collect every toy in the series. It is clearly functioning as both.

Some newer brands are even being built on a foundation of participation and promotion techniques from the outset. Threadless, for example, has limited-time promotion activities, participation requirements, and elements of a contest built right into the core of its brand experience. Also Zulily, with its daily specials and limited availability of each product offering, is a brand built on the traditional, urgency-inducing, "don't miss this opportunity" drivers of promotional marketing. The same can also be said for the pop-up retail concept Vacant, with its "here today, gone tomorrow" approach to driving visits in its markets.

Brands are also using participation strategies to develop new product ideas and line extensions. Lay's, for example, invited consumers to suggest new flavors with a program they called "Do us a flavor." Consumers voted on their favorites, with the most popular offered commercially. Following its success in the UK where it premiered, the program was rolled out worldwide, giving the company another avenue for engaging consumers, creating new prod-ucts, and pre-testing concepts,[1] all through the use of a classic promotional technique.

In this chapter, as we explore the full range of applications and benefits of participation and promotion marketing in brand activation, we will discuss the high-level strategies that will help marketers get the most out of their efforts, as well as the details of how to best select and apply tactics, including games, con-tests, and sweepstakes; cause-related promotions; tie-ins; coupons and other forms of discounting; added-value offers, such as buy-one-get-ones (BOGOs); self-liquidating, on-pack, and near-pack premiums; sampling; and more.

Our goal will be to show marketers how to use the tools of participation and promotion marketing to create engagement that both drives the behav-iors that can move more consumers toward transaction and builds the emo-tional connections to the brand that make it easier to do so in the future. The result will be achieving the full potential of these disciplines and their role in marketers' application of the AIM to activate their brands.

It is important to note that while shopper, experiential, and sponsorship marketing have traditionally been integral subsets of participation and pro-motional marketing, they are now best considered as discrete specialties due to their increasing complexity and resulting specialization as disciplines. So while they will be referenced here, they are each addressed more deeply in other chapters: shopper in chapter 4, experiential in chapter 9, and sponsor-ship in chapter 10.

THE VALUE AND POWER OF PARTICIPATION

Promotion and participation marketing strategies and tactics have long been recognized for their ability to boost a brand's immediate sales, give shoppers a reason to engage with the brand, invite deeper involvement and participation, and serve as a pivotal tiebreaker between two brands in the consideration set of an undecided shopper at the point of transaction.

Participation and promotional efforts can also, however, be powerful en-gagement drivers very early in the shopper journey, creating awareness for a brand or even taking its shoppers out of the market for extended periods via stock-up strategies and other anticompetitive techniques that can enable marketers to capture consumers before the competition even has the oppor-tunity to strike.

They also can help marketers win by more effectively igniting their organization, partners, and system. As mentioned earlier, participation and promotion tactics can help excite, educate, and motivate a company's associates, sales force, distributors, retailers, and other key constituents, to ensure that their programs are executed more effectively and therefore create greater impact with the shopper.

Given their broad potential applicability, one of the critical aspects of effectively utilizing these types of programs is understanding how to best align their tactical elements to the issues, opportunities, and objectives at each key inflection point along the path-to-purchase. Done well, the program can incent shoppers to not only continue moving toward transaction, but to even potentially accelerate their journeys and invite others to join them.

Every potential tactic has its own unique strengths and weaknesses, however, and as a result, lends itself best to different points along the shopper's journey and to achieving specific marketing goals. Beginning with those goals in mind can be a helpful way to assess the many tactical options for their power to best drive engagement in a particular circumstance. For example:

- If the goal is to drive *consideration* for a brand or to *enter the consideration set* with several similar brands, games, sweepstakes, sampling, sports and entertainment tie-ins, and offers of access can all be effective. They are all powerful mechanisms for gaining shopper attention, especially when combined with the right messaging or engagement strategy. On the other hand, offers of added value with purchase or price discounts are not as helpful in these circumstances, because, with little or no previous awareness of or interest in the brand, overall perceived relative value is not relevant yet.
- If the goal is to drive *initial trial*, offers that remove risk, such as money-back guarantees; added-value offers, such as buy one/get ones; or enabling the consumer to sample the product risk-free are typically the strongest tactics. Games and sweepstakes are generally not as effective in these situations, because shoppers typically will not buy something that they do not already desire or need simply for a chance to win some item or experience. Discounting can be an effective tactic for trial, as long as there is enough awareness and interest in the product and its value, and the discount is substantial enough to be perceived as lowering the risk of purchase.

- If the goal is to drive *trade-up* to higher-end products or more of the product, marketers might want to try offering discounts, added-value offers, games or sweepstakes, cause promotions, sports and entertainment tie-ins, or offers of access to deliver immediate value or offset the cost of the more-expensive purchase. Of course, the reason for the trade-up and the shopper's motivations need to be considered in selecting the appropriate tactic. Driving stock-up behaviors to preempt a competitor from enticing away a brand's consumers is often most effectively achieved with a simple limited-time discount or added-value offer.

- If the goal is to *cross-sell* to other related products, added-value offers, discounts, sports and entertainment tie-ins, offers of access, and sampling programs are generally the most effective in getting consumers to purchase an additional product along with their purchase of the first one, especially under the framing of creating a regimen or a more-complete or authentic experience. Like the trial goal above, games and sweeps are not as effective for the very same reason—the chance to potentially win does not create sufficient value to purchase a product or service where the baseline value has not been set yet in the mind of the consumer.

- To drive *bounce-back* or repeat visits in an accelerated time frame, the best approach is through time-sensitive, high-value discount offers or added-value offers, as well as high-value games or sweepstakes. A crucial trap to avoid: Marketers need to be sure that they do not structure bounce-back programs in such a way that rewards loyal shoppers for what they would have done or bought anyway, a flaw in many coffeehouse-style loyalty programs. They are in effect trading down the shopper, because they are giving away a free cup that would have been purchased anyway, without offering sufficient value to prevent disloyal behavior. These types of programs can be valuable to the marketer, however, if the ultimate goal is to collect transaction data that will be monetized in other ways, such as through better targeting of offers or gaining permissions to re-contact with follow-up communications.

- If the goal is to build brand *loyalty*, added-value and discount programs can be successful in driving the repeat purchases that help to instill the purchase patterns needed to build consumer loyalty. However, the issues and concerns mentioned above will need to be considered and addressed. Meanwhile, exclusive access, unique entertainment, and cause-related programs are strong at conveying the brand essence and values that align with consumers, driving them to increase affinity and connection to the brand beyond the utility it provides. One of the strengths of loyalty programs is that they can be easily customized based on the insights gleaned from the data collected, creating a feedback loop that improves the program's performance with individuals over time.

- If the goal is to drive *advocacy*, to get consumers talking, unique experiences or exclusive access to events can be powerful drivers for encouraging sharing and advocacy. This is because they can offer social currency to those granted the access that is only fully realized when shared with their friends and connections.[2] Even simple news, if it is useful or connected to a subject of interest, can get people talking. So if a marketer enables their loyalists to be in the know, that alone can motivate them to spread the word on the brand's behalf. Marketers need to be careful, however, about using incentives or rewards to drive word of mouth and other forms of advocacy, because they can diminish the quality and perceived value of the outcome.

- If the goal is to motivate and *incent the channel and internal or B2B audiences*, the tactics that are often most effective include games, sweepstakes, sports and entertainment tie-ins, and access to experiences that add high perceived value without necessarily adding the associated price tag. Of course, the prizes can and should be branded to enhance and extend the experience and remind participants about it and the brand long after the program has concluded.

INVITING ACTION AT KEY INFLECTION POINTS

Regardless of the particular situation, successful programs need a relevant offer, something that is valuable to the shopper or prospect and appropriate to the brand essence, delivered at the right time and place to incent the behaviors that move the shopper over key barriers and toward transaction. Properly constructed, these types of programs can also drive online sharing, word of mouth, and earned media that can help to further amplify the program and communicate brand features and benefits that can facilitate driving other shoppers or prospects toward transaction. To best achieve a program's full potential impact, marketers need to design them to ensure they deliver in several critical areas:

Gain Attention

The core program idea and key message needs to be big enough to break through marketplace clutter and prompt prospects to break out of their planned routines or look beyond their shopping lists to focus on the opportunity, offer, and mechanics of the program.

To achieve this objective, marketers need to think beyond the arms race of multimillion-dollar grand prizes to reach for ideas that not only get noticed, but get shared and discussed as well.

A great example is a program developed to create awareness for the resort accommodations in Australia's Great Barrier Reef. Tourism Queensland launched a campaign aptly titled "Best Job in the World," in which they offered one lucky applicant a chance to earn a salary of more than $50,000 to live in a beachside villa rent-free on Hamilton Island for six months, serving as the island's caretaker.

The only job requirements were to "work" a total of twelve hours each month feeding the fish, collecting the island's mail, and, of course, creating a weekly blog post about the experience. The caretaker was free to sail, swim, snorkel, and otherwise enjoy the island during their other 708 hours each month, posting videos that would count as time spent working on their weekly blog post.

The result: Tourism Queensland received more than $260 million in publicity about their "Best Job in the World" and its many perks, including more than 46,000 news stories, over 231,300 blog posts, and 4 million viewers who tuned in to a BBC documentary about the experience—all with a total budget of approximately $1 million.[3]

In addition to data from 34,000 applicants with proven interest in traveling to the area, Tourism Queensland achieved its real mission of establishing global awareness of the location and beauty of its islands, the first key inflection point in the leisure travel path-to-purchase.

Create Value

There are, of course, many ways to create value for consumers and shoppers beyond the financial. However, temporarily adjusting a brand's price-value equation through the use of short-term incentives can be an effective and motivating way to drive urgency and action. An added-value offer—such as a gift with purchase or a buy-one-get-one-free offer—can increase value by offering consumers more product at the same price, whereas promoting a discount or offering a coupon can increase value by temporarily lowering the actual cost of obtaining the same product or service.

Marketers can and should be more creative with offers and incentives than merely discounting a purchase price. In fact, in most cases, price discounts should be the marketer's last resort, because they can be difficult to execute in a branded way and over time can be self-perpetuating by lowering a product's overall perceived value.

The one exception to this rule is a strategically deployed sampling program. If a marketer is confident in the quality of their product and the sampling experience, offering a free sample can be a powerful way to get attention and eliminate any barrier to trial. After all, free is the best price of all, and most consumers and shoppers are willing to try a product when there is literally no cost to do so. Whole Foods, Trader Joe's, Costco, and other grocers deploy this tactic with aplomb, offering bite-size samples to appreciative shoppers who in turn find themselves spending more time in-store and adding an unplanned item to their shopping list based on the experience. Packaged-goods marketers can do the equivalent by offering small sample sizes of new products bundled with existing products as an added value, and of course, the automobile industry's extended test drives are their version of a free product sample.

Opportunities to create meaningful value for consumers and shoppers go well beyond sampling and are virtually limitless, from offering customization to increasing social good through the support of worthy causes. Value can even be found in an enhanced sense of fun and excitement during the retail experience, which is why McDonald's Monopoly games and "When the US Wins, You Win" Olympics promotions are so consistently successful.

Walmart delivered value by offering shoppers free health screenings (including blood glucose, blood pressure, and vision checks) and educating them on their health-care options under the banner of the "World's Largest Health Fair," which took place at more than 4,000 of their stores.[4] In addition to driving store traffic, the program also enabled Walmart to merchandise their organic produce and healthier food options, a strategic priority for their growing grocery business.

Another value-add can simply be enabling shoppers to demonstrate their affection—the idea Big Heart Pet Brands used to create their program "Love.

Say It with Milk-Bone," centered around Valentine's Day. Based on research that 20% of the population would prefer to spend the holiday with their dogs, yet only 13% of dogs received a treat on that special day, the campaign promoted Milk-Bones as the first-ever valentines for dogs with special "Love" biscuits hidden in Milk-Bone packages that offered the pet a chance to win treats for life.[5]

Premiums or gifts with purchase are another great way to create value. The cosmetics industry does this frequently, with free makeup bags or brushes offered with some specified minimum purchase. This is most effective as a trade-up strategy, enticing an already-interested shopper to spend just a bit more to get the free premium. The premium, however, needs to be of interest and value, and consistent with the image of the brand it is promoting, to take advantage of this tactic's brand- and business-building power.

On the B2B side, the French railway system, SNCF, created a game to attract engineers that required contestants to solve a series of mathematical and scientific challenges. They promoted the program on their website, via social media, and on posters at 180 engineering schools, attracting 5,000 players[6] who loved a challenge simply by adding value to the job search experience and application process.

All of these programs were not only effective at creating value that reached and engaged their targets, but they also amplified the programs' impact by creating talk value and social sharing.

Build the Brand

At the very minimum, promotion and participation ideas need to be in alignment with the brand's essence and core promise, and ideally should be uniquely ownable by the brand and reinforcing of its key attributes. Marketers can design programs to build their brand while building their business by keeping the following screens in mind when developing and approving program concepts:

- **Branded Voice:** Once a brand's essence is defined, its expression needs to be developed with equal precision, and the brand's tone of voice is a critical aspect of it. Too often, however, the voice of the brand, even when clearly defined, can be ignored or overlooked in service of creating program elements obsessed with being urgent and loud. If the style and language of a brand is conversational and forthright with a touch of humor, for example, then the program elements need to be the same. The invitation to engage in the program is an invitation to engage with the brand, and the voice with which that invitation is delivered needs to reflect it.

- **Branded Proposition:** The concept and structure of every program also need to emanate from and be consistent with the brand's purpose and core values. If a brand's mission is to help customers live better lives, then its programs should not only connect to that mission, but actively reflect the values and priorities of the brand. As a result, a program with a game mechanic could feel frivolous and inappropriate to such a weighty mission, whereas a contest focused on doing good in one's community could be perfect. In contrast, if a brand is about bringing fun into people's lives, then its programs can and should be fun for its participants. Participation programs are an opportunity for prospects to experience an aspect of the brand—whether it is the brand's attitude and values, or its benefits and product features. As a result, even the prize, offer, or opportunity should help to advance the brand's positioning and communication of its core promises, and any retail partners, sponsored properties, and spokespeople need to reinforce the same.

- **Branded Theme:** Falling from the branded proposition, the promotional theme should also support the brand—and even communicate the brand promise or its key attributes. Oreo launched a program with Meijer called "Discover What's Inside," reinforcing a core aspect of the product. Likewise, when Walgreens launched "Walk with Walgreens," a program that rewards shoppers for walking for better health, the theme not only reinforced Walgreens' health-focused positioning, it also promoted one of their key competitive advantages: walkable neighborhood locations.

Drive Engagement across All Channels

To maximize impact, marketers should not simply default to replicating the same message across all communication channels, but instead should optimize their messaging by channel in order to more effectively move prospects to engage and ultimately move closer toward transaction. The goal is not only to communicate the right message at the right place, but to also utilize the unique strengths of each medium to fullest advantage based on where the shopper is in his or her journey.

Programs typically have several layers of information that will need to be communicated, from simple awareness of the opportunity and reasons it should be of interest, to details on how to participate and specifics on how to maximize and share that experience. To try to accomplish all of these objectives at every point of contact, or to just communicate the same single message at every interaction, would be inherently ineffective. To use McDonald's Monopoly game as an example, the exciting grand prize and impressive quantity of lower-level prizes need to be understood and of interest to a new potential participant before details of how to collect game pieces to win are even relevant.

As discussed earlier, television and radio can be effective media for creating initial awareness and interest, and driving people in-store or online to find out more. Once online, marketers can provide more-detailed information, such as rules, prize pools, and participating locations, and create opportunities to inspire advocates to post or share their experiences with others. Sequencing the messages to maximize interest and minimize friction will drive a deeper level of engagement quicker, and ultimately result in a more enjoyable and effective program.

Enable Partner and System Execution

A program is only as good as its execution. As a result, marketers need to consider all of the stakeholders across all channels and what is needed to educate and motivate them at each execution point. In the case of Monopoly, the prizes and program can be compelling and loved, but if a store manager fails to put up his store's signage, his customers may not even know the program is running until after they have ordered. That is why marketers may run games or contests within their games or contests, such as awarding the store manager with the best in-store display, to motivate maximum participation and proper implementation.

Marketers essentially need to treat each channel player at each execution point as a separate internal audience, using all of the appropriate participation and promotion techniques to get them excited about the program and clear on how to deliver their role in it to ensure optimal execution.

Keep It SMART

By definition, an effective sales-building program must be SMART: Specific, Measurable, Attainable, Relevant, and Time-Bound. SMART goals are used in performance management, HR development programs, and in academia when writing and assessing student learning and performance outcomes.

As applied to participation and promotion programs, SMART means that the goals of the program must be *specific*, meaning clear, concise, and concrete; the results of the program must be *measurable* based on the marketer's key performance indicators (KPIs), whether it is year-over-year sales, traffic, redemptions, or some other criteria; the goals must be *attainable*, keeping in mind that an overly aggressive program can doom success just as a too-conservative one will not produce optimal ROI; as for *realistic*, the program must have the proper system support, a workable timeline, and other realities in place to ensure its successful implementation; and, to create urgency, the program must be *time-bound*, with a clearly communicated end date.

Marketers should keep in mind these SMART criteria when evaluating all aspects of the program, including its objectives, offers, mechanics, and measurement plans, as well as integrating the other AIM criteria above to ensure that the program aligns with the marketer's goals and is constructed for maximum impact, to most effectively build their brand while also building its sales.

TIME TO BE EXPERIENTIAL

Now that we have discussed participation and promotion marketing approaches and how to unlock their full potential to activate behaviors among prospects, as well as key constituents, let's turn to an area that was born from promotion marketing, but has evolved to become its own specialized discipline: experiential marketing. Long recognized as a powerful tool in driving behavior change, it has become even more potent thanks to the ubiquity of digital technologies and social media. Join us to discover the activation power of experiences.

9

Are You Experiential?

As the proliferation and sophistication of digital, mobile, and social platforms continues to grow, it may at first glance appear ironic that the value of concrete, real-world experiences continues to grow as well.

Interestingly, the most digital- and social media–oriented of generations, Millennials and Gen Z, place an extremely high value on obtaining experiences, particularly those that are unique or exclusive and aligned with their interests and values. They even go so far as to value experiences over material possessions. In fact, research conducted by Harris found that 78% of Millennials would rather use their money to go to a "desirable experience or event over buying something desirable."[1]

What is an apparent dichotomy between physical experiences and social media is actually more of a synergy, as it turns out that unique and exclusive experiences are the ultimate currency of social media. The more social media–obsessed people have become, the more they are recording and sharing their experiences via real-time photos and videos. Selfies, of course, are the prime example, focused on documenting that "you were there" prior to sharing with friends and generating comments and discussion. The more often experiences are seen and shared, however, the more others want to do the same, and the more value truly exclusive experiences begin to have. As a result, the actual value of the experience increases beyond simply the individual's time during the experience, to include the social currency of sharing it.

It is this dynamic that is making experiential marketing—such as events, pop-up retail locations, guerrilla marketing stunts, sampling events, and other forms of physical experiences—all the more engaging and potent. As a result, marketers are able to utilize them to increase transaction counts, capture valuable data, build affinity with a brand, encourage consumer opt-in to loyalty programs, increase earned media and word of mouth, and, ultimately, realize increased sales and profits.

For today's consumers, every touchpoint is an experience—from online to off-line, and from retail to social and beyond—and they expect to move seamlessly between all of them. Any hiccups in the quality and consistency of their interactions while moving between environments can erode the brand equity and trust built up over time. In contrast, when brands deliver consistently meaningful, memorable, and valuable experiences across channels, consumers will reward them with not only time and attention, but with affinity, loyalty, and advocacy that will reverberate across their social interactions.

In this chapter, we will look at experiential marketing and how it can be an increasingly powerful tool in activating brands and driving behavioral change. We will discuss how to fully utilize this often-siloed discipline by integrating it with the rest of the marketing mix, enabling it to more effectively align with social media, retail marketing, and other critical disciplines to better drive consumer activation, improve results, and enhance overall marketing ROI.

While today's consumers do not tend to differentiate between on- and off-line experiences, for the purposes of this chapter, we will define experiential marketing as the industry typically uses the term, as the discipline focused on actual real-world events and interactions, even though they may often be enhanced through the use of mobile, social, and other digital technologies.

NAME YOUR OBJECTIVE

Experiential marketing is a tremendously versatile tool and can play many roles in activation, both building brand and driving sales, as well as motivating the various stakeholders in the system, such as employees, trade, distributors, retailers, and more. One of its fundamental strengths is that it can help marketers boost brand affinity, sales, and ROI across the entire path-to-purchase, from the upper funnel to the point of purchase.

In the upper funnel, for instance, shoppers with no previous connection to the brand could be engaged with compelling events or experiences of such value that they would happily opt in to receive future communications, creating the foundation for personalized content and behavior-driving incentives going forward. In this case, experiences can leverage the passion points of the target, such as music, fashion, sports, or other forms of entertainment. Additionally, shoppers may be offered a chance to sample the brand during the event at no cost or risk, enabling them to "try before they buy," to begin understanding the brand's features, and then assigning value to them.

In the lower funnel, experiential can drive already aware and engaged shoppers further into the brand by creating experiences that help marketers close the deal and drive transactions. These shoppers may be offered the opportunity to enjoy a sneak preview of an unreleased product or to sample it in new and exciting ways. The automobile industry's use of ride-and-drive events is a great example, where engaged shoppers may be offered the opportunity to test-drive the brand's car on a race track and do the same with several competitive models, all without needing to visit competitors' showrooms.

Across the funnel, consumers can enjoy unique experiences that reinforce key attributes of the brand, subtly (or not so subtly) educate participants on brand features or benefits, and provide them with uniquely sharable assets that can enable them to broadcast their amazing experience with the brand across social media, providing potential future consumers with the social proof or testimonials they may need when researching a purchase, as well as the validation they may crave post-purchase.

Experiential marketing can help marketers drive engagement and address the key inflection points that can hinder or accelerate the shopper's journey toward a transaction, wherever those points may be. Specifically, marketers should actively consider the tools of experiential marketing to deliver:

- **Brand Awareness:** Just simply breaking through the clutter to remind lapsed consumers and inform potential prospects that a brand exists can often be enough to drive many of each to begin their journeys down the path-to-purchase toward incremental transactions. Experiential marketing can help to create that awareness, because it can be a powerful way to not only attract attention, but also convey and reinforce the brand promise. Its power extends beyond just those attending the experience to include those who hear about it via traditional, earned, and social media before, during, and after. For an example, consider the impact that Heineken experienced when they had the band TV on the Radio play in front of one of their bill-boards in Manhattan. With very little pre-publicity—the concert was not announced until three hours before it began—the event drew more than 5,000 people and gained wider exposure through both traditional and social media channels. The YouTube video of the event alone reached more than one million views. With the brand top of mind, immediately following the concert Heineken Light sold out in the bars near the location, and that following quarter sales of the brand jumped 22% in New York City.[2]

- **Sampling Opportunities:** From small events in the parking lots of grocery stores to large ones such as Lollapalooza or the Super Bowl, experiences can provide marketers with captive crowds of like-minded individuals who might be interested in trying the brand, establishing an association between it and an experience they value. Attendees can be reached on their way to an event, during it, or after, depending on when and where the marketer identifies as optimal for prospects to sample the brand. Marketers should always make sure to pair sampling activities with the distribution of some form of incentive to purchase the brand at a later date, in order to leave the prospect with a reminder of the brand, capitalize on positive sampling experiences, lower the barrier to initial purchase, and help track and attribute transactions to the sampling opportunity. Marketers should also build in reasons and opportunities to capture and share the experience on social media. The Unilever ice-cream giveaway mentioned in chapter 5 was at its core a sampling program, enabling people to try flavors through an engaging use of technology—in this case, a vending machine that distributes a free product with facial recognition of a smile. The machine made it easy for participants to share their unique sampling experience with others by enabling them to share the photo of their smile directly to their social graph via Facebook, extending the program's reach and the brand's association with happiness.
- **Product Demonstrations:** Particularly helpful for newer or complex products, experiences can give marketers opportunities to demonstrate or explain how their products work and spotlight key features and benefits. They also can provide attendees with the chance to ask questions and receive usage instructions, which can reduce the product's perceived complexity and counter any intimidation by the required learning curve, lowering a potential barrier to purchase prevalent in the technology space in particular. As the saying goes, "Seeing is believing," and it becomes even more powerful when attendees can

go beyond sight and sound to actually touch and try the product as well. Of course, product demonstrations are also good opportunities to incent purchase and create urgency through special offers limited to the duration of the event. Product demonstrations can be successfully conducted at concert and sporting venues during the extended downtime prior to the actual event, as well as at pop-up experiences, transit stations, grocery stores, malls, festivals, and other shopping venues, as well as at trade shows for B2B audiences.

- **Education:** Experiences can also help current users of a product or service increase their affinity for and loyalty to the brand by educating them on how to get more out of it. Educational or coaching experiences can be used to introduce, reinforce, or extend concepts, procedures, or processes related to the product or service, for example, giving attendees in B2B situations for example, new skills that make them more valuable to their employer, and as a result, increasing their loyalty to the brand. Educational experiences can be seen most often in the B2B world, where detailed knowledge is often critical for the user, and the price and profit margins justify the time and expense of providing these types of more in-depth opportunities. Technology and software-as-service brands utilize these approaches, creating engaging and memorable learning opportunities for new or casual users that both increase their proficiency with the brand's products and their impression of the brand as a high-value solution provider. When the value provided is substantial enough, some of these experiences can pay for themselves or even become profit generators. Adobe, for example, offers events such as The Summit Digital Marketing Conference, which includes three days of workshops and training on their products, for which participants pay upward of $1,800.[3]
- **Loyalty:** Rewarding brand loyalists with access to hard-to-get, exclusive, or unusual experiences—such as tickets to sold-out concerts or sporting events— can help spark their advocacy for the brand, driving valuable word of mouth as well as endorsements. To make the experiences even more valuable, memorable, and sharable, marketers can plus them up with notable features such as backstage passes, one-of-a-kind seating, or meet-and-greets with event stars. Marketers need to be careful, however, because, as mentioned in the previous chapter, there can be a fine line between the perception of a reward and a bribe. The goal is to make the loyalist feel special and provide them with social currency that they want and choose to share. The rest is up to them.

FIGURE 9.1

The Ad Council created an event and used it as online content to educate people about bias. The consistent tagline they used on each piece read, "Before anything else, we're all human. Rethink your bias at lovehasnolabels.com."

Source: R/GA

- **Retail Promotions:** Experiential efforts can help launch in-store promotions by creating awareness for the program as well as driving traffic to the store and other retail access points. As a result, they can also help curry favor and build stronger relationships with retail partners in situations where the marketer distributes products through others. Experiential programs can also create added value for the retailer's shoppers, to the benefit and pleasure of the retailer, by enhancing store visits with entertaining shopper experiences that may include samples, demos, and other unexpected experiences. The win for the marketer, of course, in addition to building their relationships with key retail partners, is a location for their event with a built-in audience already in transaction mode. By varying these types of events specifically to the retail account, marketers can highlight different aspects of their brand depending on the known interests and demographics of the retailer's shopper base, creating more-targeted and -effective experiences.

- **Content:** Experiential marketing can create powerful synergies with content marketing approaches. Events can be employed for the delivery of live content of interest to the target and related to the brand's product or category—the non-selling, information strategies discussed in chapter 6. Additionally, the event itself can be a content creator, in the form of videos, photographs, testimonials, and other sharable artifacts generated from the experience that can be used to drive engagement with others. In many ways that is the strategy the Ad Council used with the creation and distribution of their "Love Has No Labels" campaign, a program designed to educate people about bias and expose them to their own. To create content for a video, the Ad Council had various couples hug behind a faux X-ray screen in a shopping mall in Santa Monica, California, on Valentine's Day 2015. The effect to bystanders was an image of what looked like skeletons embracing, until the couples came out from behind the screen to reveal to onlookers their varying identities, genders, races, and, in some cases, disabilities, driving home the point that love is love, regardless of the labels. Once edited, the video of the event was posted on YouTube and Facebook and promoted through PR and media, generating more than 40 million views in just two days, and at last count, more than 100 million combined views worldwide.[4] In this case, a video of an experiential marketing event designed for social media placement and coupled with PR efforts achieved what brand advertising traditionally did best—changing attitudes as a precursor to changing behavior.

So while experiential is effective at driving action and behavior, it can also play a role in shifting attitudes, creating awareness, driving consideration, and building affinity.

- **Lead Generation:** Events and other experiences are optimal moments to generate leads and capture data for the sponsoring brand, which can be utilized in the delivery of targeted content and incentives following. Marketers should plan ahead, however, to ensure that they gather the information that will enable them to qualify, quantify, and prioritize the leads generated and have in place the infrastructure to promptly follow up on them while the experience is still fresh in prospects' heads and hearts. The lure of a unique experience—whether it is a free sample of a product, exclusive access to music or entertainment, or a personal encounter with a luminary or celebrity—often has sufficient value to motivate a prospect to share some basic information to participate. Marketers need to understand that value equation, and make sure they take full advantage of it, without going too far in their quest for information and turning away the very people they are trying to engage.

- **Earned Media:** As we demonstrated when discussing how experiential marketing can generate and serve as content itself, creatively conceived and executed experiential programs can generate media coverage as well. This is yet another instance where integration between agency disciplines is critical to optimal success, as marketers need to coordinate with their PR firm while planning and developing programs through their experiential partner. Pop-up events, stunts, and guerrilla tactics can often generate broad coverage if appropriately planned. Adidas's vertical soccer stunt is a classic example. In it, soccer players suspended by cables over a Tokyo intersection played soccer on a vertical field painted on a billboard, and the media took it from there.[5, 6] To maximize coverage, marketers should endeavor to ensure that members of the media are in attendance at the actual event itself, if at all possible. After all, media professionals are human, too, and given the opportunity, they can get caught up in the emotion of an experience as much as the general public.

- **Recruiting:** Just like the digital program for the US Navy mentioned in chapter 5 and the promotional marketing program for SNCF in chapter 8, experiential can also be a very helpful tactic in the B2B marketing challenge of recruiting new employees and other company stakeholders. It can be a particularly powerful tool in recruiting volunteers and supporters for not-for-profits and other social causes. The reason is *social proof*,[7] namely that people tend to look for direction in the behavior of others to see what is normal and expected, particularly when the way to behave is uncertain or ambiguous, and when the others are seen as being similar to them. Since experiential events can help people to see that others are supporting a cause as well, they can become more willing to make a greater personal investment if the organization's goals align with their own beliefs.

- **Employee and Stakeholder Performance:** Because of its high perceived value, the promise of experiential rewards can help motivate behaviors among employees and other stakeholders in companies' organizational systems, from those in the channels to those on the sales floor representing the marketer's brand to various prospects. Experiential opportunities can enable marketers to offer incentives—such as private concerts available only to employees and other one-of-a-kind experiences or trips to exotic locations—that recipients value at levels well beyond their actual costs. These experiences also tend to be remembered, treasured, and recalled more than other more tangible rewards, driving greater affinity with the recipient and increased word of mouth among others.

In virtually every case, incentives for activating appropriate follow-up behaviors by participants should be included as part of each experience, helping to guide participants over key inflection points and along the path-to-purchase. Depending on the marketer's overall goals for the experience and the inflection points the experience is designed to address, these incentives can motivate the prospect to try, trade up, add on, or simply share an artifact from the event. What's more, events can often achieve more than one objective, for example, creating overall brand awareness through social media while driving loyalty with current brand advocates and leads from new prospects in attendance. A stunt can generate mass media attention while rewarding high-value customers and system stakeholders who are given privileged access. Of course, with each program, the marketer needs to establish clear, SMART objectives, so the results can be effectively analyzed and the impact clearly understood.

EXPERIENCE BEST IN CLASS

While experiential tactics are very versatile, they need to be utilized strategically, deployed based on insights into the path-to-purchase, and targeted against specific opportunities to influence key inflection points along the way—just like every other marketing discipline.

In the previous chapter, we explored how participation and promotion marketing—long considered the business-building side of the equation—can also be utilized to help build brands. Much of this same thinking can be applied to experiential marketing efforts, as well.

For an overall roadmap, marketers should start by identifying the key inflection points along the target consumer/shopper/prospect's path-to-purchase, as is critical to applying the AIM. Once those points have been identified, the marketers or their partners can begin to develop experiential opportunities that would create sufficient value at those points to engage the target and address the selected barriers or opportunities. Once the marketer has identified an experiential concept consistent with or complementary to the brand, the concept can be designed and developed to guarantee the optimal user experience; to ensure that data capture and branding opportunities are fully leveraged; and to properly establish the measurement framework to evaluate effectiveness and optimize for future iterations. The marketer can then execute each touchpoint and asset of the experience with the aforementioned in mind, making sure to include incentives for future follow-up behaviors by experience participants.

This rigor is critical, as experiential marketing programs need to be carefully designed and executed from beginning to end to ensure that the experience creates the desired effect for the participant and builds their connection to the brand. In many ways, it is analogous in effort and focus to creating a complex online experience; every bit as much time, thought, and attention needs to be invested in planning and designing the user experience off-line as is spent on creating experiences online.

Each aspect of the event's execution must be precisely managed, from the invitation to participate, the admission to the experience, and navigation through it, to the facilitation of the event staff, who are walking embodiments of the brand as far as participants are concerned.

Specifically, marketers must initially engage their prospects by getting their attention and inviting their participation through the value and appeal of the offered entertainment, access, cause, or even utility aspects of the experience. When the prospects attend, the experience itself must be carefully branded and clearly ownable so as to put the spotlight on key aspects of the brand and memorably bring them to life.

As a result, developing the user experience (UX) and environmental design of the event is critical to effectively manage how attendees move through the physical space and fully leverage the power of the experience to activate the brand. Marketers should think about designing their experience in "4D"—that is, a three-dimensional space that people move through over time, the fourth dimension. Key points to consider include the sequence of the overall messaging to enable a frictionless journey for the participant; the opportunities for branding, in particular at ingress and egress, to facilitate the participants' recall of the association between the brand and the activity; the integration of technology to aid navigation, so the activity seamlessly corresponds to the brand's other on- and off-line experiences; and, perhaps most importantly, points where the brand and the participant can integrate and utilize mobile to engage more deeply and/or share more easily.

The marketer needs to actively enable and facilitate the documentation of the experience by the participants so they can easily share and promote it on social media to increase the program's reach. Those efforts should include creating ways to help memorialize the event by providing artifacts visitors can retain to relive the experience and potentially utilize in off-line word-of-mouth opportunities. Of course, in planning for the documentation and memorialization of the experience, marketers need to ensure that the opportunities they create and the items they provide reinforce or convey the key brand attributes of the experience, so the effort continues to build the brand while helping to drive sales.

If possible, and consistent with objectives, the event or experience can and should be designed to be inherently newsworthy to help enable earned media exposure beyond social. This can be a powerful amplifier, because when an event is covered in the press, online, or on television, it often spurs additional social media sharing by providing individuals with additional content to share, link to, comment on, and discuss. Additionally, when an experience is covered by an objective third-party source, it creates the kind of social proof that increases the perceived value of the experience by those who attended, providing them with additional social currency, and, as a result, further incentive to share. Additionally, of course, earned media mentions can help increase brand awareness, reinforce brand attributes, and drive interest and sales for the sponsoring product or service among those who were not in attendance.

Last, what data the marketer chooses to capture, and how, needs to be planned at the user-experience stage, as this will be critical to fully leveraging the experience's ability to enable and enhance future marketing efforts. If data capture is not planned for early in the development process, there is the risk that valuable learning opportunities may be overlooked, or at the very least, not as seamlessly integrated as they could be if they are bolted on after the initial user-experience planning stage. As in all marketing disciplines, the ability to capture critical data that can be applied across the marketing spectrum is essential when it comes to more effectively impacting behavior, boosting ROI, and reinforcing key brand attributes. Experiential is no exception.

SOME EXPERIENTIAL OPTIONS

Marketers should be cognizant that any experience they create should be treated as an extension of the brand itself, and therefore needs to deliver the same personality, tone, look, and feel as an individual would experience online, in the retail environment, or during the user's other interactions with the product or service.

With the growth of experiential marketing as a discipline, however, there are several types of tactics that have emerged as some of the more commonly utilized, including:

- **Pop-up Retail:** With little or no publicity—and often promoted solely on Twitter or other social media—these temporary store environments open quickly and often close just as fast. They give consumers the excitement of discovery and drive immediate action because of their very limited time of availability. Once cutting-edge, even Target has employed the tactic, briefly opening a pop-up store in Rockefeller Center years ago to promote a new women's clothing line by Isaac Mizrahi.[8]
- **Product Previews:** During these efforts, high-value customers, members of the media, thought leaders, and other key influencers are invited to the sneak preview of new products or services so they can experience them before everyone else and build broader interest by sharing their scoop with others. Think of it as the front row at a Fashion Week runway show or the live launch of the latest Apple product. Limiting initial access creates more

excitement among those outside and more social currency for those inside when they share their experience with others.

- **VIP Events:** Great for engaging individuals and fueling sharing of their experience with others in their social graph, VIP events reward high-value, loyal customers through access to exclusive functions and other experiences one would not be able to obtain on one's own. Think about events such as these as the after-party following the Fashion Week show mentioned above.

- **Behind-the-Scenes Experiences:** This gives lucky winners, high-value customers, thought leaders, bloggers, and other social influencers a chance to see something that others typically do not. Think of this as being on the set of a television show or movie while it is being shot, or being seated in the kitchen of a high-end restaurant. Exclusive access bestows a sense of insider status on the attendee that not only creates positive sentiment, but also an incentive to share it.

- **Entertainment Events:** From sponsoring concerts, sporting events, and other properties to creating one's own, entertainment experiences offer an opportunity for access that has high perceived value. They also give participants the kind of social currency and documentation that can fuel postings on social media.

- **Education/Training Events:** In the B2B world, educational events provide value to attendees by enabling them to attain continuing education units (CEUs), required in many fields, while providing value to marketers by enabling them to better explain how to use their products. However, they can also be successful tactics for B2C brands as well. For instance, a high-end cutlery brand might host cooking classes, underscoring the need for and benefit of its products, while enabling better experiences through its proper usage. In these types of experiences, the opportunities for content creation and content marketing can be great.

- **Stunts:** Designed to drive earned media via press and social sharing, these are one-off events that might have very few attendees, but tremendous reach, earning back their investment through the broad exposure they generate. For example, the TV on the Radio mini-concert on the Heineken billboard mentioned earlier could be considered a stunt. It attracted only about 5,000 attendees—too few to generate a meaningful increase in sales of beer—but a lot of media attention, even outside of New York City. In this case, it was these secondary exposures that helped boost its ROI.

- **Mobile Tours:** When marketers endeavor to reach new prospects—potential consumers who do not generally patronize them or their retail partners—they may choose to launch a mobile tour that travels to key markets. Often utilized for distributing samples or demonstrating new products, these mobile units— usually tour buses or tractor-trailers with some form of slide-out expansion capability—can transform into mobile showrooms, functioning kitchens for food products, or other experiences at high-traffic locations such as college campuses, sporting events, and more. The trucks are often scheduled to also visit the parking lots of retail partners, driving traffic and awareness, and as mentioned earlier, helping to curry favor with the retailers. Mobile tours can be expensive to create, but the ability to build it once and then visit multiple locations over time can create efficient payback.

- **Sponsorship Ambushes:** Here the marketer stages an experience that creates the impression the brand is a sponsor of a high-profile event without actually being one (and without paying the associated fees). Sponsorship ambushes can include offering product samples, distributing free premiums (particularly wearables that recipients might don at the event to create additional awareness), or conducting product demos to attendees on their way to an event sponsored by a competing brand. In one well-known example, Nike ambushed the World Cup in 2010 in Mexico with the experiential program Nike City Cup.[9, 10] Taking advantage of soccer excitement prior to the World Cup, Nike created an event that enabled local teams to compete to be crowned City Champions during the World Cup festivities, increasing awareness of Nike with soccer-obsessed teens during the World Cup without actually being an official sponsor.

- **Guerrilla Events:** These are low-cost street activities that create awareness, engagement, and earned media, but, unlike the sponsorship ambushes above, do not imply that the marketer is sponsoring an event. For a period, flash mobs were a popular guerrilla marketing tactic, but examples of the genre can get more innovative and elaborate. FedEx Kinkos hired an actor to sleep on a desk in a high-traffic commuter train station in Chicago to promote the idea that they are enabling the end of the all-nighter.[11] When Volkswagen launched The Fun Theory campaign in Sweden, they went even further: They turned a train station staircase into piano keys, one per step, so commuters could make music as they walked up or down, inspiring people to use them instead of the escalator; they put sound machines into garbage cans, so people would hear strange noises when they threw away their garbage; and they created a traffic camera that rewarded people who followed the speed limit, among other experiences—all to promote the fun and environmental friendliness of Volkswagen.[12, 13]

LEARNING FROM EXPERIENCES

While experiential efforts can clearly play important, powerful, and varied roles in brand activation, some of the best practices from experiential marketing can and should also be leveraged more broadly across other marketing disciplines. Experiential marketing's focus on architecting an experience end to end to make each point of engagement memorable and, if possible, inclusive of artifacts worthy of sharing, is an approach that can benefit digital user experience design, direct, retail, and content marketing as well.

Additionally, experiential marketing's endeavor to not just talk about the brand and its promised attributes, but to instead work to literally bring the brand to life, as illustrated by the Volkswagen example above, has broad applicability across the marketing spectrum. Many of the discipline's best examples move beyond simply creating an attention-getting stunt to enabling prospects and other key audiences to actually experience key aspects of the brand, from the explicit utility of a product to a set of attitudes or values that both the brand and its users embrace.

Finally, as is so critical to any successful experiential program, marketers across disciplines from retail and social to promotion and PR need to devote the same focus to training, equipping, and motivating any consumer-facing employees or associates who serve as brand ambassadors so that they will become a walking embodiment of the brand—conveying the brand's essence and values in every aspect of the performance of their jobs.

A perfect example is the legendary brand stewardship provided by the flight attendants at Southwest Airlines. The brand clearly conveys its essence, attitudes, and values to all employees and applicants, so they will express the same essence, attitudes, and values to the brand's customers. Even Southwest's recruitment materials convey their brand values; for instance, on their careers homepage, they state: "At Southwest Airlines we connect people to what's important in their lives—that also means connecting our employees to what's important in their lives!"[14] When marketers embrace the language, attitudes, and personality of their brands in communications with employees and other key stakeholders, it can help encourage them to do the same with their customers.

To better understand another marketing discipline that can bring tremendous value to the others, come along to the next chapter where we examine an area that is often closely aligned with experiential: sponsorships.

In this chapter, we will explore how sponsorships can create, enable, and advance valuable brand experiences, how to gauge the quality of fit between marketer and sponsor, how to leverage sponsorships to help build activation programs across other key disciplines, and how to get a true measure of ROI and results. The outcome will be a working knowledge of how to ensure that sponsorships are worth the investment by deploying them in the ways most effective in driving brand activation.

Now a Word from Your Sponsor(ships)

Sponsorship marketing typically excites an organization, but it frequently delivers less than optimal results for the marketer. The reasons are myriad, but more often than not, they can be traced back to treating the sponsorship as an end in itself, rather than as an enabler of the marketers' broader strategies and objectives. So why, as one of the oldest marketing tactics, is sponsorship marketing currently in vogue to the tune of $20.6 billion a year in North America alone, and still growing?[1] After all, it seems every major marketer and most minor ones are engaging in some sort of sponsorship marketing activities.

The reason is that, if utilized correctly, sponsorships can create real value for consumers in ways that drive engagement, incent behavior change, and reinforce key brand attributes. Marketers may be aware of the potential benefits sponsorships offer, but many are in need of an approach that enables them to more fully take advantage of those opportunities by utilizing them more effectively as a strategic part of their broader marketing efforts. That is precisely where the AIM can help.

Sponsorships can be leveraged to not only drive engagement and value, but also to create relevant content, experiences, and even new communications channels that can reach targets at critical points along their paths-to-purchase. Through the AIM's more methodical and interconnected approach, marketers should be able to unlock five critical brand- and sales-building opportunities nascent within most strategically selected sponsorships.

First, sponsorships offer an opportunity to engage the passions of an established fan base that follow the sponsored athlete, sports franchise, or sporting event; the musical artist; entertainment property; worthy cause; community event; or other property to create awareness, interest, affinity, and participation with the brand. While sponsorships utilize a form of borrowed interest, they can still enable a brand to communicate its values, attitudes, and points of view to a passionate group of consumers, while also potentially dramatizing the brand's key features and benefits through the association itself, as well as through its ancillary communications in paid, earned, and owned media channels. As long as the borrowed interest is synergistic with the brand and does not overshadow it, it can be a powerful and telegraphic way to drive awareness, involvement, understanding, and affinity for the brand, in the same way that entertaining plotlines and evocative imagery can be borrowed to drive interest in traditional broadcast advertising. When there is a strong overlap between a marketer's target audience and an area of passion, such as music, sports, or fashion, a sponsorship can provide a powerful opportunity to cut through the messaging clutter with a topic of proven interest and emotional appeal to the target.

Second, sponsorships can help to create brand news that gets attention from consumers, partners, and key stakeholders—not only through the association itself, but also via the resulting program, its promotional or participation offer, and its potential impact on the brand's consumers, channels, distributors, retailers, and internal audiences. High-profile properties with passionate fan bases often create newsworthy sponsorship opportunities that can help to reinvigorate a brand and its product in the marketplace, opening eyes and minds to taking a fresh look. In all communications associated with the sponsorship, the marketer needs to strategically demonstrate the alignment between the brand and the property to highlight and build on the association, and counteract any potential perception of a tacked-on marketing ploy. By properly leveraging the kind of news and brand halo that a well-chosen sponsorship can create, the marketer can help to spark, grow, or reignite interest in the brand, even in the absence of new product innovations, line extensions, or other substantive changes that traditionally create word of mouth and social sharing.

Third, sponsorships can enable a brand to create timely, relevant, and sharable content valued by an already established fan base that can be powerfully deployed at key points of contact to drive engagement with consumers and shoppers. The brand can utilize elements or assets from the sponsored property or deliver new information about the participation programs or events built around the sponsorship. The content can take a variety of forms to effectively engage its audiences—from text, video, audio, and photographs to games, news, trivia, and more—as long as each communication conveys key attributes and values of the brand to build interest and affinity. The content can be utilized as a door opener for the marketer to drive initial engagement or sharing, or it can be the reward for participation or purchase, depending on the content's type, value, and where it is most powerfully utilized along the shopper's journey.

Fourth, sponsorships can give marketers the opportunity to create unique or exclusive experiences that can drive engagement directly with the brand and its products, as well as generate sufficient interest and value to incent participation and enable other communications. In the process of negotiating a relationship with a sponsorship property, it is important that the marketer not just focus on the placement of their logo within the sponsored property's communications, but also identify and obtain access to experiences and opportunities that can be utilized in promotional and participation activities. These kinds of exclusive experiences can range from tickets to sneak previews and premieres, and backstage access or exclusive seating at sponsored concerts and events, to meet-and-greets with stars, appearances in a film or television property, and other unique, behind-the-scenes opportunities. These types of experiences can often be easily negotiated in advance, as they are likely already in place for media, opinion leaders, and other VIPs, but they can be nearly impossible to achieve after the fact. That is why it is critical that the marketer identify opportunities of interest and potential ways to leverage the sponsored property early in the process when negotiating leverage is at its greatest and the desired experiences are not already allocated.

Finally, sponsorships can also enable the creation of high-value artifacts that consumers can desire, keep, and use to remind themselves of the brand, the property, and the associated experiences long after the program has ended. Consider McDonald's Happy Meals toys and their featured sponsorship properties that change approximately every month—or the collectible glasses and other items that many soft drink or quick service restaurant brands offer. Consumers seek them out, collect them, and use them because they love the properties they represent, but they also serve as constant reminders of the sponsoring brands that enabled the initial and ongoing experiences associated with using the items.

So as marketers continue their shift from building brands to fully activating them, sponsorships' abilities to connect with people and their passions, as well as deliver inherently sharable social content, are only going to make them an increasingly important weapon in brands' marketing arsenals. To achieve optimal results, however, marketers need to move beyond simply aligning values and building associations with these properties to more fully utilizing their power to effectively drive engagement and change behavior.

Let's explore the many opportunities that sponsorships provide and how marketers can leverage them to build more robust and effective brand-activation programs. We will discuss how to gauge the quality of fit between the marketer and the sponsor brand, how to get a true measure of ROI and results, and how to ensure that the sponsorships selected are worth the investment. But let's first consider the different types of sponsorships and compare their relative strengths and weaknesses.

FOUR KEY PROPERTY CATEGORIES

As sponsorships continue to grow, marketers have a robust and growing range of options from which to choose. To help simplify the many and varied opportunities, however, sponsorships have traditionally fallen into one of four different areas:

Sports

The options here extend from sponsoring leagues, teams, and athletes to experiences at the stadium during the game day, championship tournaments (or subsets of them), team meet-and-greets, fan conferences, tryouts, drafting events—even naming rights to the stadium. In fact, virtually any time the sports team or property is active, there is a sponsorship opportunity.

Of course, with sports, there is always an element of uncertainty. A cherished athlete can be injured or caught doing something unsavory on or off the field, and in an instant, an entire star, team, or league's prospects and profile can change. The sponsored team can win or lose, and weather can play a deciding factor in the outcome of a high-profile event and the related sponsorship. In many ways, however, that is part of the appeal of sports and a real opportunity for smart marketers who are ready and equipped to take advantage of the uncertainty. When combined with fans' passions, this uncertainty can inspire fans to display their team pride (with marketer-sponsored wearables), cheer on their team with pregame rituals (including marketer-sponsored brands), or engage with the property and the brand in other creative ways before, during, and after the moment of truth.

Even simple endorsements can require the same type of strategic planning and consideration as a sports sponsorship. In these situations, the athlete (or sports celebrity) is typically lending his or her name, brand essence, attributes, and credibility to support the brand, or is in partnership with the marketer in creating a co-brand. Because of these similarities, many of the strategies and approaches presented in this chapter, as well as the overall AIM process, can be applied to more fully leverage endorsement opportunities as well.

Entertainment

From sight and sound to smell and taste, entertainment sponsorships offer marketers the opportunity to create a wide range of experiences to engage consumers—from sponsoring concerts, tours, festivals, and speeches to demonstrations, films, television shows, celebrity events, and many, many others. Entertainment sponsorships have moved well beyond the traditional options of movie premieres and concert tours to include sponsoring celebrity chefs and their reality-based cooking competitions, and overt (as well as covert) product placement deals.

In the B2B world, brands are sponsoring high-profile keynote speakers and even secondary presenters at key industry trade shows, as well as sponsoring entire conferences, book tours, webinars, and other education, thought leadership, networking, and social events. Each of these avenues provides powerful branded opportunities to reach identifiable targets seeking new experiences, connections, insights, and knowledge, as well as opportunities for the brand to become associated with those experiences, connections, insights, and knowledge without having to actually produce them.

Entertainment properties and industry events have built their business model on driving sponsorship relationships, so it is important to understand where there are—or are not—opportunities for the marketer's brand to differentiate itself. Cookie-cutter sponsorship packages can help a marketer quickly reach the right audiences, but there is the real danger of making a large investment to simply wind up in a sea of logos at the bottom of a poster or piece of collateral without achieving much else. When a target audience sees a sponsorship relationship as short-term and interchangeable, marketers need to seriously evaluate if they are actually creating any brand value or driving any meaningful level of engagement. When a measure of strategically focused creativity is brought to the sponsorship discussions, however, a win-win scenario can be developed between sponsor and property that often not only reduces fees to near zero, but can also lead to some truly breakthrough brand activations in market.

Kraft's Crystal Light Liquid partnered with Zynga's Words With Friends to create a first for the popular mobile/social game by enabling all of its fans across the country to play together in the same game at the same time.[2] This first-ever use of an HTML5-based Words With Friends Facebook Challenge mode created news for both brands and brought Crystal Light's new liquid line extension, and a valuable trial-driving offer, to the attention of Words With Friends fans everywhere right on their phones, resulting in one of the brand's most successful product launches ever.

Causes

With consumers' growing demand that brands possess a moral compass that aligns with theirs,[3] supporting a worthy cause through the sponsorship of events connected to it can help consumers to understand and experience the brand's values and priorities, while delivering an emotionally resonant incentive for engagement and participation. Marketers must be forewarned, however, that consumers want to know that a brand is authentic in its actions and beliefs, and truly practicing what they preach and sponsor. Ignoring the need to be aligned and truly authentic in words as well as actions can result in a backlash on social media and a negative impact on brand equity, not to mention lost transactions.

A cautionary case in point was the trend of companies jumping on board to convey their support for environmental causes, only to generate much broader exposure for the resulting charges of "green washing" when they were accused of joining a movement in name only, rather than actually putting real efforts behind it through their corporate practices.

Properly selected and embraced, however, cause-related sponsorships can provide marketers with an opportunity to not only create broader awareness for their organization's good works, but to also activate engagement among key targets that build the business while building the brand. As we have seen in the Coca-Cola Arctic Home examples in chapters 2, 6, and 8, and the #forRMHC example in chapter 5, sponsorships can enable consumers to more easily engage with and support the causes they already love through their involvement with the brand, so the brand, cause, and consumer become aligned. The result is that consumers, as well as the brand and cause, are able to experience value from the engagement beyond the mere utility of the brand's product features. This can drive both immediate and longer-term shifts in consumer attitudes and behaviors, as well as an increase in social sharing as a result of the positive associations with all parties doing good while doing well.

Community

A strong feeling of belonging is a key emotional driver of humankind as a whole,[4] and brands can play a meaningful role in enabling vehicles for its creation through the sponsorship of community-building, educational, and civic projects that generate goodwill and awareness as a result. Examples range from the creation of parks and playgrounds to the support of community centers or schools in the locales where the brand operates or does business.

Marketers can utilize the association with these community institutions to not only drive affinity, but to also drive visits and purchase behaviors. For example, as more and more communities host family-friendly, alcohol-free New Year's Eve celebrations, brands have the opportunity to sponsor the efforts, utilizing retail outlets as distribution points for tickets, or even arranging for their products or packaging to be used as the tickets themselves. Simply providing complimentary products or services to the event can turn the sponsorship itself into a sampling opportunity that directly reaches new potential customers.

While community sponsorships tend to be local, they can be executed at a national scale. Kellogg's Frosted Flakes' Plant a Seed campaign featured a national program with local community impact through their offer to help rebuild local community ball fields.[5] It generated both national awareness and local engagement as communities nominated and voted for their neighborhood fields to be selected.

In these types of sponsorships, the brand can use its media advertising to communicate the need for the project and its involvement, and through a strategic use of other marketing disciplines activate a range of behaviors from conversations on social media that coalesce an online community, to retailer participation in promoting a program where a percentage of purchases or profits will be donated to advance consumer-selected community-building efforts.

DRIVING BEHAVIOR WHILE BUILDING THE BRAND

So how do marketers best utilize sponsorships, partnerships, and tie-ins to drive behavior change and reinforce the brand? The first key is to look beyond the typical objectives of reach and affinity, and leverage the sponsorship's ability to create unique and motivating value for consumers, an objective that can be achieved by employing the inherent appeal of the property to create unique opportunities for:

- **Providing Access:** These include the tickets, meet-and-greets, behind-the-scenes experiences, and more—the options are essentially limitless. Wherever people desire access, a sponsor can come to the rescue. In a fairly typical example of this kind of execution, Citi, as the sponsor of Billy Joel's one-concert-per-month ongoing run at Madison Square Garden, offers their cardholders the ability to purchase tickets before they go on sale to the general public. Additionally, Citi enables their VIP cardholders to have a picture taken with Billy Joel (in front of a Citi-branded backdrop, of course), so attendees can memorialize their experience and share it on social media, further extending the program's reach.[6]
- **Creating Experiences:** Continuing with the Billy Joel sponsorship example, Citi also created a special, branded lounge on-site for their VIPs, featuring an open bar and appetizers. To broaden the experience's reach via official artifacts that can be shown and shared, the VIPs get credentials on arrival and can also take and print out photos from a photo booth in the lounge. Of course, the booth also enables the VIP to share those photos via social media, letting the individual's friends know about their experience, as well as the sponsor of it. Executions like this have become fairly standard in event sponsorships, but they illustrate the approach, and smart marketers can use them as a springboard for creating more innovative and unique brand experiences.
- **Enabling Self-Expression:** Whether it is through the development of custom co-branded T-shirts or other unique ways of demonstrating their interests, values, and passions, providing consumers with creative avenues

FIGURE 10.1
Tic Tacs transformed their mints to look like Minions, enabling fans to interact with the property.
Source: barefoodblogger.wordpress.com.

to interact with a sponsored property utilizing its key equities is a great way to drive engagement and sharing. Coca-Cola, as a sponsor of the World Cup, wove together 3.5 million fan-submitted photographs of themselves to create a gigantic flag—the world's largest composed of a mosaic—which was themed "The Happiness Flag," and revealed at the start of the 2014 competition in Brazil.[7] The self-expression can also involve the brand's product itself. Consider Tic Tac's tie-in with the Minions movie. As part of the relationship, Tic Tac transformed their little mints to look like mini Minions, an activity that fans of the *Despicable Me* franchise had been doing on their own.[8] Through this minor, temporary product change (printing distinctive faces onto the already Minions-shaped candies), they enabled fans to creatively interact with the product and characters, turning Tic Tacs into temporary toys that empowered fans to express their love of the brand and the property in their own unique way.

- **Sharing Knowledge:** Knowledge is power, and helping to spread the wealth is a common approach in B2B marketing. The *Harvard Business Review* (HBR), for example, regularly offers free webinars and publications featuring prominent academics, business leaders, and authors that are sponsored by ADP, UPS, Citrix Go To Meeting, SAP, and other firms that want to reach management professionals and be allied with HBR and the themes of the presentation. With the increasing popularity of content marketing, other examples abound. For instance, virtually every marketing executive receives a bevy of e-mail invitations from media outlets inviting him or her to attend webinars sponsored by B2B marketing technology (MarTech) brands or data and technology suppliers. Once an executive chooses to view a webinar, he or she will likely receive a targeted e-mail or follow-up contact from the sponsoring brand, offering additional content or seeking to set up a sales call. In this case, sharing knowledge is a way to not only build the brand, but also to generate and qualify leads.

- **Contributing to Social Good:** Sponsorships that enable people to feel they are making a difference in the world can be powerful drivers of engagement, and we have seen many examples of that approach in action. From Kellogg's Plant a Seed to Coca-Cola's Arctic Home, programs that make doing good simple play to people's altruistic and selfish instincts at once. In the case of Arctic Home, those who believe in the conservation of polar bears or the work of the World Wildlife Fund can feel that they are helping a worthy cause merely by purchasing Coca-Cola products or donating the points they had already earned through My Coke Rewards to the cause-related program.[9]

TO THE SPONSOR GO THE SPOILS

By creating value using the approaches above, sponsorships can help the marketer build consumer connections to their brands while the consumer is engaged by the opportunity to build connections with the sponsored property. Microsoft Bing's sponsorship of the release of Jay Z's autobiography is an excellent case in point. Aiming to increase visits and intent to use among an audience that was younger and more coastal than their middle-aged, Midwestern core users, Bing created a culturally relevant opportunity for entertainment, access, and unique experiences all in one. Using a digital gaming experience built on Bing's Search and Maps, they offered millions of Jay Z fans the ability to assemble his autobiography before it hit stores by discovering its pages in unique media spaces around the world. The offer not only increased Bing's relevance to its target audience, but it also drove behavior: in this case, actual trial of the product, as the game required the use of Bing's Search and Maps functionality to play.

Bing reported that visits to its site increased by 11.7% during the campaign,[10] a jump that was achieved without the support of other advertising during the program period. What's more, by driving trial—and therefore overcoming the lack of familiarity that can be a critical barrier to usage and adoption—participants reported that they planned to continue using Bing even after the game.

This sponsorship was successful because it remained focused on clearly defined goals and worked on multiple levels. Bing and Jay Z created value and participation with consumers that drove them to engage with and potentially rethink their attitude toward the product. What they also did—which is critical to maximizing the value of any sponsorship, but particularly one that may have multiple partners—was to create territory within the sponsorship itself that uniquely accrued affinity and equity to the marketer's brand: in this case, positioning Bing as the vehicle of discovery of the most highly valued content in one's areas of passion.

As the Bing program and earlier examples show, when properly conceived and executed, sponsorships can deliver sufficient value to consumers to capture their attention and incent a click, share, visit, trial, trade-up, add-on, or opt-in. To begin improving the effectiveness of sponsorship programs to build both their brands and their business, marketers should start with the following:

- *Review the objectives.* Marketers need to determine which of their existing marketing goals or strategies a potential sponsorship can help them realize and what key shopper inflection points it will help them address, instead of developing new objectives to fit and rationalize the potential sponsorship.
- *Identify the equity opportunity.* Marketers must determine the brand space they can actually own with the help of the sponsorship, and what they can achieve with it. By clearly identifying the equity opportunities, marketers can then proactively seek out the right sponsorship opportunities instead of waiting to be pitched by properties seeking to recruit partners. Being proactive can help marketers to identify opportunities before they are widely available and ensure that their brand will not get lost in large sponsorships that have multiple partners.
- *Assess the potential partner's equity fit.* There is nothing worse than partnering with a property that does not align with your current brand or where you want to take it. Make sure your partner will enable you to reach a key target and reinforce—or define—your brand essence and equities. In assessing the fit, marketers should seek to determine alignment with the target shopper and consumer in interests and values, as well as with the marketer's brand essence, personality, values, and brand behaviors. Note that both alignments need to be authentic. Consumers are savvy and can tell when a sponsorship seems forced, or has been manipulatively or cynically undertaken.
- *Explore the opportunities.* The marketer, of course, should also explore the brand's needs along the path-to-purchase and the support a sponsorship

could provide to help address those inflection points where the brand could attract or lose potential shoppers and consumers. It could be early in the journey, by helping the marketer create awareness of the brand, at the end by providing consumers with an incentive to repurchase, or anywhere in between. As part of this assessment, the marketer needs to consider costs and timing, by comparing the sponsorship costs and budgets versus the potential and realistic upside, as well as evaluating the timing of the sponsorship in relation to the brand's marketing needs.

- *Understand and value what the sponsoring brand brings to the table.* Every successful sponsorship helps both partners. Jay Z's Facebook page increased by one million fans during the Bing promotional period,[11] which helped his book reach #2 on the *New York Times* bestseller list the week after launch. Marketers can use the value they bring to the table to negotiate their partnerships, potentially lowering licensing fees and securing additional marketing opportunities. Often, marketers can even create win-win scenarios for both parties where little, if any, money changes hands—while both the brand and the sponsored property achieve their individual objectives.

- *Look for ways to activate the sponsorship across all relevant channels.* By understanding all of the ways a brand's shopper moves toward transaction, the marketer can utilize the sponsorship to create maximum value and impact key behaviors. For instance, the marketer can utilize the sponsored property to not only create awareness of the brand and communicate a key brand attribute, but also to activate their sales force, retailers, distributors, and internal departments through the use of the sponsorship's appeal and opportunities to create value—all of which can boost ROI.

- *Determine the sponsorship's role in your marketing calendar.* A sponsorship can be a short one-off program, a yearlong relationship, perennial, or even evergreen, when the brand realizes long-term equities through the association and the property ultimately becomes ownable by the marketer as a branded event. McDonald's annual Monopoly game is a great example. Customers have now come to expect the program, as it has become a regular, recurring part of the brand experience. Still highly anticipated, it helps to drive incremental restaurant traffic during the sponsorship period, spotlights select menu items, and promotes a motivating prize pool that gives the brand negotiating power in obtaining them.

- *Capture data and measure results.* As with the rest of the AIM, clear objectives will enable the marketer to fully embed opportunities for data capture, measurement, and optimization, which will be critical to quantifying and improving sponsorship ROI moving forward. The marketer should create opportunities to utilize captured data to learn more about the interests and motivations of its shoppers and consumers, so the brand can more effectively drive future interactions through better-targeted incentives and more-relevant content. By focusing the sponsorship on a clearly defined inflection point along the shopper journey, as discussed above, the marketer can also more effectively measure the sponsorship's impact and results by tracking the desired behaviors—be they inquiries, traffic, trial, or trade-up—relative to costs, to ultimately quantify and evaluate ROI.

As we have seen, sponsorship marketing can offer much more than mere affinity and "eyeballs." It can play a starring role in activating consumer behavior and motivating an entire system to help do the same. People's passions—whether they are causes, sports, music, movies, or something else—truly offer a myriad of opportunities for engagement, content, sharing, and value. When marketers find the right match, they can fully unlock the power of the partnership to build passion, business, and brand equity.

SPONSORSHIPS' PROPERTIES
The insights and best practices from sponsorship marketing offer valuable lessons that can be applied more broadly across other marketing disciplines, including the following:

- Look for synergistic opportunities and win-win partnerships in every appropriate marketing program, because these enable the company to build both the brand and business while potentially lowering the overall marketing spend. Of course, the first place to seek synergistic opportunities is with retail partners and those in the channels by aligning with their objectives and understanding their priorities, which is a key principle of shopper marketing as well.
- Look for opportunities to leverage shopper and consumer passion points that align with the brand in all of the content and experiences the brand delivers to help drive optimal engagement. From brand advertising and

digital to experiential and content marketing, understanding and aligning the brand with the interests of its shoppers and consumers can help to drive engagement across virtually every marketing discipline.

- Find a uniquely branded way to communicate and engage. Even in the borrowed interest world of sponsorships, marketers can build both the parent brand and its equity into the sponsorship program while also building sales and profits. The same can be true for any other touchpoint or context as well.

Perceptive readers are undoubtedly starting to see how the currently fragmented marketing disciplines can interconnect to create synergies, and how the best practices of each can be applied to the others to boost both brand equity and ROI.

Before we close the loop in the final chapter with how to manage the integration of all of the various marketing specialties, let's take a brief look at one of the fastest-growing marketing disciplines: branded journalism and PR. In this next chapter, we will look at the third leg of what has been called the paid, owned, and earned triad, as well as how the changing world of journalism is bringing powerful new opportunities that marketers can use within the context of the AIM.

Build Your Relationship(s) with PR and Brand Journalism

It is no surprise that like other legacy marketing communication disciplines, including advertising, direct response, shopper marketing, and sponsorships, the field of public relations (PR) has continued to evolve its unique core capabilities, strategies, and tactics. So it should also come as no surprise that public relations, a discipline known for helping to shape what people think about a company, brand, or personality,[1] can play a vital role in inspiring individuals to take action.

Public relations draws much of its power as a component of brand-activation efforts by bringing together its unique understanding of how to create credible, sharable content with expanding social listening capabilities and the ever-increasing ability to speak one on one with consumers and influencers. It also brings along with it a broader corporate perspective, helping C-suite executives craft and deliver a wide range of messaging that can be useful in aligning internal and external stakeholders in service of activating brands. In contrast to traditional advertising and other marketing specialties, which tend to focus on the purchaser and those in the channel, audiences for PR efforts can range from employees, investors, and other corporate stakeholders to NGOs, regulators, government officials, and, of course, the media, opinion leaders, and (particularly during crises), the general population.

Likewise, the use of brand journalism, a form of content marketing that focuses on the creation of news- and feature-style content by marketers, is also playing a powerful role in the world of brand activation.[2] HubSpot, in their downloadable booklet, *The CMO's Guide to Brand Journalism* by Dan Lyons, pointed out four main strategic uses for it: creating brand awareness, delivering industry news (augmenting the capabilities of independent trade and consumer media), displaying thought leadership, and generating leads.[3]

In this chapter, we will explore the many ways that public relations and brand journalism can be utilized in brand activation to most effectively build a brand while also building its business. Since we have already discussed social media and other disciplines that can be found within PR firms, we are focusing this chapter on the classic or legacy areas of the discipline. While content marketing has been addressed in chapter 6, the newer approaches of brand journalism will be explored here, because of their unique intersection between journalism and public relations.

By properly integrating select public relations strategies and tactics, and emerging brand journalism approaches into an overall activation effort, the marketer can enable key audiences to encounter relevant brand messages in additional ways and forms at critical inflection points along their path-to-purchase.

What is more, brand journalism—like other areas of content marketing—can also enable marketers to identify leads and offer them pertinent follow-up messaging when it is most needed and effective. As a result, properly employed, PR and brand journalism efforts can make a difference between suboptimal and optimal marketing ROI.

WHAT'S THE STORY WITH PR?

Claudia Strauss, CEO of Grey New York Activation and PR, believes that just as most effective brand-activation programs need to have a component that drives social media, which we explored in chapter 5, most should also contain an angle, idea, or tactic that amplifies the overall reach by driving earned media with traditional and/or key influencer outlets.[4] To achieve either or both, the marketer will need PR expertise and support.

"At my agency, PR is often called 'the secret weapon,' and PR teams are included in briefings, throughout idea development, and through execution, whenever possible," says Strauss.[5]

These types of messages can also be conveyed through content marketing efforts with the channel, distributor, and retail partners, and reach the general public directly through postings on the marketer's websites, as well as through Twitter, Facebook, and other venues. These placements, however, often work as a self-referential echo chamber that can help fuel media coverage, since journalists scan Twitter and other sources when seeking new ideas or additional content for pieces they are currently researching.

Of course, PR and social should work hand in hand, as mentions across the spectrum of media outlets can drive additional postings and mentions on social media, as well as vice versa, creating an effect that can surround key prospects with relevant brand exposures. As an example, recall Heineken's TV on the Radio program mentioned in chapter 9. While the mere presence of the pop-up concert drove social sharing, the event also earned mentions by the media, providing additional third-party content for those who experienced the event, as well as other fans of Heineken and/or TV on the Radio, to post and share.

Or consider Grey New York's Cannes Lions Award–winning work with an organization called States United to Prevent Gun Violence (SUPGV) that was designed to inform Americans that, contrary to popular belief, having a firearm in a home actually increases the risk of injury or even death for everyone living there. Grey New York and SUPGV wanted to drive behavior change as well, namely that shoppers would decide not to purchase a firearm.[6] To maximize ROI, they knew they needed to efficiently cast a wide net, and PR was just the discipline for the task. So Grey's PR team played a crucial role throughout the entire program, starting at the ideation stage and continuing through the rollout and resulting media discussion.

"PR professionals should always have a seat at the table" when ideating activation campaigns, said Strauss, adding that "PR professionals are attuned to creating sharable content that can reach multiple audiences."

The activation idea at the heart of the program: a pop-up gun store in New York City.

The unique twist: All of the guns for sale were involved in shootings—and some even in mass shootings—all of which was detailed on the hang tags of each gun, as well as by the sales representative who described the gun's features.

On the surface, the pop-up gun store was an experiential event. But keeping it in the realm of a pure experience would have meant limited reach and suboptimal results. Instead, the PR team worked hand in hand with the production team to ensure that hidden cameras captured the shocked reactions of shoppers as they discovered a gun's history, and then used that content to

FIGURE 11.1
A pop-up store in New York City that sold guns with criminal histories as part of a PR campaign sponsored by States United to Prevent Gun Violence.
Source: Grey New York.

create a video that they forwarded to key media influencers when soliciting coverage. The PR team oversaw the editing of the footage to ensure that the final video would be as effective as possible in getting the broadcast media's attention. They also invited local, New York City–based media representatives to visit the store in person, so they could understand firsthand how easy it was for anyone to buy a gun.

Through their targeted efforts, the story grew, enabling the pop-up gun store to gain substantial national and international media attention. In one example, they were able to convince Rachel Maddow to dedicate nearly ten minutes of her cable news show to the story, which in turn drove additional coverage. The results: The video of the hidden camera footage received more than twelve million online views during the first week alone;[7] 80% of the shoppers who visited the store changed their mind about buying a gun; and the organization received a 3,000% increase in donations, among other successes.[8]

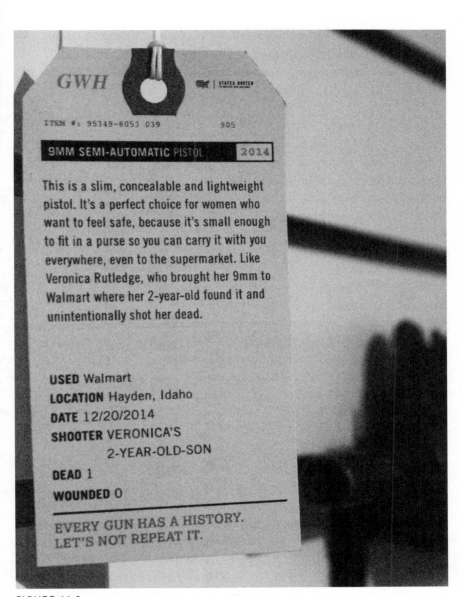

GWH

ITEM #: 95349-6053 039   905

9MM SEMI-AUTOMATIC PISTOL   2014

This is a slim, concealable and lightweight pistol. It's a perfect choice for women who want to feel safe, because it's small enough to fit in a purse so you can carry it with you everywhere, even to the supermarket. Like Veronica Rutledge, who brought her 9mm to Walmart where her 2-year-old found it and unintentionally shot her dead.

USED Walmart
LOCATION Hayden, Idaho
DATE 12/20/2014
SHOOTER VERONICA'S
                    2-YEAR-OLD-SON

DEAD 1
WOUNDED 0

EVERY GUN HAS A HISTORY.
LET'S NOT REPEAT IT.

FIGURE 11.2
The hang tags described the guns' features and history.
Source: Grey New York.

As this campaign and the Heineken TV on the Radio event examples both underscore, PR as part of the third leg of the paid-owned-earned media triad can be a powerful component of a multichannel campaign designed to drive behavior—from selling more of a particular brand of beer to enabling social change.

Contrary, however, to some popular marketing books designed to promote the use of PR strategies and tactics, when creating an activation campaign, marketers need to keep in mind that the "free" media of PR and the owned media of their content marketing efforts are not actually free, and do not necessarily replace paid advertising or other marketing efforts that include executional costs, such as experiential and sponsorship programs. Rather, in brand activation, PR typically works best synergistically with the marketers' other efforts, each amplifying and broadening the reach of the other, particularly when the role of each is fully understood in relation to the others.[9]

For example, paid and owned media can be guaranteed, of course, while earned media cannot. Paid and earned, however, will be seen, because they are external to the brand, while owned has no such certainty, and often needs to be promoted (unless discovered by organic search). As mentioned earlier, but important to emphasize, earned media is perceived as more credible, because of its implied third-party endorsement, while consumers typically view paid and owned messaging as inherently biased and focused on promoting the self-interest of the brand.

Because of these benefits and drawbacks, marketers need to strategically balance all three to most effectively and efficiently achieve their objectives and reach the intended audiences at the appropriate times. Regardless of that balance, the marketer's PR strategies, ideas, tactics, and messaging, just as with their approach to social media and other marketing specialties, need to emanate organically from the brand and the overall marketing concept, and not merely be a box check that completes some imaginary list of expected marketing disciplines.

To maximize the effectiveness of their brand-activation efforts, marketers need to follow the same methodical approach to utilizing PR as they do with all of the other disciplines discussed so far, and should not deploy these efforts simply because a specialist is readily available or because the competition or broader marketing world is using them. Rather, the use of PR strategies and tactics in brand activation, as with all of the other marketing disciplines, must put consumers and shoppers at the center and originate from an identified need or opportunity to add value at key inflection points along their paths-to-purchase that helps create movement toward the desired behavior or transaction.

THE POWER OF PR

The difference between legacy advertising and PR was best summed up by Richard Pinder, CEO, London and International, Crispin Porter + Bogusky, in a piece he wrote for *The Drum* about advertising and PR coming together. "Advertising's heritage is in the notion of disruption to gain audience versus PR's end-goal of earning the audience's trust."[10]

With that in mind, PR as a discipline has several key strengths that can be helpful in creating brand activation.

First, as acknowledged earlier, PR offers the power of third-party credibility that can enable a brand to generate word of mouth. In fact, brand stories in the news media can provide the type of social proof that makes a message feel particularly real and important, which, in turn, can help to fuel sharing and, ultimately, a movement. For example, let's take another look at the ALS ice-bucket challenge. Three factors made that effort accelerate so quickly:

- *The unique engagement idea.* The social challenge of either pouring a bucket of freezing ice over oneself while recording the event for social media or writing a donation check to the ALS Association (most of the donors probably did both) created human interest and an element of fun, attracting over seventeen million participants in the first year alone.[11]
- *Social media as fuel.* The use of social channels was built directly into the mechanics of the challenge. As participants were preparing to pour a bucket of ice over their heads, they called out other individuals to do the same, providing a one-to-one social lever that spread the message, and increased the number of participants who also posted their responses. Celebrities also got into the act, posting their challenges (see sponsorships), which further raised awareness, added credibility, and attracted the news media, which amplified exposure and sharing further (while promoting the celebrities' brands as well).
- *Local and national media hook.* While the challenge was primarily fueled by social media, it was first reported by local media in the Boston area—the home city of Pete Frates, a former professional baseball player who has been

diagnosed with ALS, who originated the idea.[12] The locally relevant story was then picked up nationally, thanks to the fun and entertaining video clips created, giving the challenge the momentum it needed to go viral.[13]

As this case demonstrates, an engaging idea, social media, and traditional media can all work together synergistically, and, as a result, the ALS Association received 2.5 million donations totaling $115 million in the first year of the challenge alone.[14] In these types of programs, it is, of course, the role of the PR professional to help tailor the idea for maximum media appeal, seed the content in the online world, and bring the program to the attention of all pertinent media outlets, from traditional print, TV, and radio to blogs, podcasts, and more.

Another strength of PR, as we saw with both the ALS Challenge and the pop-up gun store campaigns, is that once a story gets picked up, it can offer a relatively large reach at a comparatively small overall cost. Marketers need to remember, however, that to be effective, PR activities need to be ongoing. This not only helps to keep the brand top of mind, but also helps the PR professional build key relationships on behalf of the brand, which increases the likelihood of the journalists being receptive to covering a story when it becomes available.

A PR colleague of ours, Matt Carlson, compares this relationship building to dieting or staying healthy.[15] Like losing body weight or maintaining optimal health, building strong PR relationships, whether they are with the traditional media or emerging players, does not happen overnight. They need to be built and cultivated bit by bit over time, requiring a long-term mind-set and ongoing investment, which needs to be incorporated into annual budget planning for PR-related costs.

As we have discussed, integrated PR efforts need to be organic to an overarching brand idea and not feel like a tacked-on bid to generate extra attention. Just as marketers need to understand the priorities of their retail partners to create successful shopper marketing programs, so, too, do they need to understand the priorities of the journalists, bloggers, or other media prospects, as well as the editorial styles of their intended outlets, to achieve real public relations success.

A third strength, particularly relevant to brand activation, is that properly structured PR programs can uniquely enable the demonstration of key brand ideas in authentic, non-advertising environments. PR professionals can help to develop video news releases and other promotional elements, such as the hidden camera video created for the pop-up gun store, designed to inspire coverage on news programs and websites. They can help train subject-matter experts to provide quotations for print-based media and sound bites for television or radio, as well as appearances on select news and talk shows. The impact of having these third-party endorsers speaking articulately about a product's features or a brand's values, versus a marketer creating messaging about the same in advertising and other sponsored media, can be exponential, particularly as it relates to credibility and social proof. Additionally, marketers can then package those appearances into video and audio sound bites that can be shared socially or with additional media outlets for further message amplification.

Finally, as noted earlier, PR practitioners traditionally have also provided crisis management services when required by marketers and brands. While every effort should always be made to think through every aspect of a marketing program and anticipate all contingencies beforehand, occasionally problems may arise that can create unintended consequences for brand activation. The marketer, therefore, should always develop a crisis communications plan before a program launches and budget for crisis management support if needed, whether via in-house specialist or outsourced partner, to mitigate potential impact to both the brand and business should something go awry. In the event something does not go as planned, the marketer should strive to be the first to tell the story, with as much transparency as possible, so the brand can control the narrative to the greatest extent feasible.

The goal, of course, is to address potential roadblocks at key inflection points on a consumer's path-to-purchase. As a result, negative social media comments that do not affect prospects, shareholders, government officials, or other stakeholders are often not worth the time and effort to address in a brand-activation context. In fact, research shows that publicly shared negative comments by one person can actually lead others to adopt the brand. First, these comments can create awareness,[16] particularly for new products.[17] They can enhance the believability of the positive reviews[18] (another study showed that "68% of consumers trust reviews more when they see both good and bad scores"),[19] and the feature being reviewed might not be important to the particular purchaser.[20]

Crisis management best practices can, however, be applied even when issues are not extreme. By acting responsively to social listening and media monitoring, community managers and other PR representatives have the opportunity to address negative comments in real time and proactively educate media and influencers, so they have the information they need to communicate positive messages about the brand. After its bankruptcy, GM worked with its PR firm to operate a centralized news bureau to ensure the circulation of positive stories about the company's products and progress.[21] Similarly, Arby's deployed brand supporters when they launched their limited-time Smokehouse Brisket sandwich to counteract media influencers skeptical about the sandwich's quality, enabling Arby's to launch their most successful promotional product in the company's history.[22]

A crisis management approach can also enable marketers to take advantage of news and other real-time developments to help build the brand and activate prospects. Consider when the stadium lights went out during the 2013 Super Bowl, and Oreo responded with a tweet that proclaimed "You can still dunk in the dark." Created on the spot by Oreo's digital agency,[23] it was the PR principle of immediate responsiveness in action that enabled relevance, awareness, and success, in the process resetting expectations for how to conduct true real-time social media messaging. By applying the principles of traditional crisis communications, including predetermined approval processes, checkpoints, and messaging principles, marketers can utilize a system for responsive message delivery that takes advantage of real-time events and leverages them to the brand's greatest advantage.

CREATING MEDIA OPPORTUNITIES

Once the key shopper inflection points are identified and the brand program idea is defined, marketers need to identify the optimal PR tactics to help support their goals. Some common options include:

- **Guerrilla Events:** The marketer can create a happening, event, or experience so unique and newsworthy that journalists will want to cover it, such as the TV on the Radio / Heineken example. Another approach worthy of note was an effort in 2014 to promote the third season of the *Dallas* reboot on TNT, for which Grey New York developed a pop-up gas station in Manhattan that undercut competitors by nearly two dollars a gallon. "We brought TV's most famous family, the Ewings, into the real world by blurring the lines between fact and fiction," Strauss wrote. When ideating the program, they aimed for coverage "across a broad spectrum of media, from entertainment to auto and everything in between," a metric they easily surpassed. They also leveraged Facebook posts, viral video messages by John Ross Ewing, and a sweepstakes giving fans the chance to win a custom Black Gold Card with a $50 balance. Together, the effort utilized the news of gasoline prices the country had not seen in decades to evoke nostalgia for a bygone era and the hit show associated with it. As this example illustrates, the key criterion for success is that the guerrilla event be both newsworthy and convey branded messages that would activate or engage the shopper, consumer, or prospect at relevant points to impact their behavior.

- **Celebrity Endorsements:** The goal here is to create awareness and/or credibility for the key message via an endorser who is a category expert, tastemaker, or celebrity who would believably have passion for the brand. When utilizing an endorser strategy, the celebrity's noteworthiness should create the news power that will result in media appearances and mentions. Often the endorser will also be used in advertising and other messaging, creating a consistency of brand association across all channels, as well as to offer consumers, prospects, or key partners exclusive access to the endorser to help generate additional awareness and coverage.

- **Implied Endorsement Photo Opportunities:** Often combined with the use of celebrity spokespeople, or executed through a product placement strategy including the use of swag bags filled with branded gifts, this PR tactic enables consumers to see various notables holding, using, or talking about the marketer's brand. Of course, when a celebrity is spotted using a brand's product on his or her own, marketers can try to take advantage as well. One way is to simply thank the celebrity via social media by reposting the image. The marketer just needs to be careful to find the right tone to ensure that the celebrity stays favorable to the brand and does not feel that his or her notable status is being exploited inappropriately for the brand's gain.

It is important to note that all of the PR options above can be utilized to reach beyond the most established media players to also connect with category bloggers, citizen journalists, YouTube celebrities, and other influencers. Regardless of the approach or form of amplification, when managed effectively, PR has the power to augment brand-activation efforts by creating awareness of a participation program or experience, driving consumers to digital channels to learn more, creating social proof that can inspire both purchases by those considering or advocacy by those who already have, building credibility for a brand or program, and creating a sense of mass and scale for a brand or its efforts.

There is one more key strategic point to effectively integrate public relations into the marketing activation universe: The best practitioners understand the journalistic side of the business, enabling PR efforts to intersect with the world of content marketing. But it is not just PR practitioners who are getting into the marketing act. Professionals trained as journalists are joining them as well.

BRIEFLY ON BRAND JOURNALISM

Traditionally, in news channels, the marketing side and the media or journalistic side were kept as separate as church and state. It was a distinction that was sacrosanct. Journalists needed to remain impartial, no matter how fervently PR specialists tried to influence them. Now, however, professional journalists are being brought into the marketing arena. Whether it is as a moonlighter still working for a legacy or online publication, or as a full-time writer for an agency or brand, journalists are creating content to appear as native advertising in commercial publications or as stories in publications owned by the brand or its parent, but with limited association to them. For native advertising, the piece will look and feel like the surrounding editorial, but will be strategically created to advance the aims of the sponsoring marketer. As a result, publications and broadcast outlets selling native advertising are essentially returning to practices that were common more than a hundred years ago.[24]

For the marketer, these practices are essentially an extension of their content marketing program, which we explored in chapter 6, but there is a difference. Content marketing, which includes some native advertising, has the goal of explicitly moving prospects toward transaction, while brand journalism is less tied to driving prospects to purchase.[25] Rather, its role is to convey stories that advance the brand experience and brand engagement without explicitly promoting the brand. For example, an aspect of the American Express Open campaign focused on creating and sharing articles about what it's like to manage a small business, thereby showing that American Express understands the concerns of owners of small businesses without directly saying so.

Another role of branded journalism is to lay the groundwork and prepare the greater societal narrative for the branded communications to come, so the public will be more receptive to the eventual messages. To be successful, a marketer's narrative must fit within a larger group narrative in order to feel true to its audiences and align with their predispositions or understandings of common sense. Brand journalism can be utilized to help shape that larger narrative, laying the foundation that will help audiences be more receptive and interested when they encounter similar topics, ideas, experiences, opportunities, or products offered by the brand.

For example, as part of the launch of the 2015 season of *House of Cards*, Netflix hired *The Atlantic* to produce a story exploring the relationships between US presidents and their wives. Notice that the story did not explicitly talk about *House of Cards*; instead, it merely created interest in a related topic to the benefit of the brand messaging to come. In another instance, to help promote a series produced by Amazon Studios called *Bosch*, about a detective in LA working to solve a cold case, Guardian Labs developed for *The Guardian* what they claimed was the first piece of investigative brand journalism by exploring a real unsolved murder to spotlight aspects of detective work.[26]

With brand journalism or native advertising, the content blends into the surrounding stories and feels like the other editorial around it, implying that it has the credibility of the outlet. It is this believability, along with the content's storytelling ability, that gives the piece its power. As a result, there are certainly situations where the simple, engaging storytelling of a brand journalism strategy can help to reach prospects and engage them in a way that ultimately helps move them closer to transaction, and therefore, the technique should at least be in the consideration set of marketers focused on activating their brands.

BRINGING IT ALL TOGETHER

A theme throughout the Activation Imperative Method is that all of the marketing disciplines need to and can work in concert with each other to maximize effectiveness, and that the best practices of each can have broader applicability across the others. Through the explorations of the best practices of each discipline, it may have become apparent that many are tactically complementary, and can be effectively aligned on a strategic level. Now we are going to make that alignment explicit and explore how to coordinate all of the disciplines into a cohesive effort that boosts marketing ROI.

Join us as we bring *The Activation Imperative* to the end of its path and outline an actionable approach to activating brands that represents the next step in the evolution of effective marketing.

AIM for Optimal Activation

There are myriad reasons why marketers or organizations may not be fully activating their brands and target audiences.

Many may be focused on marketing objectives that they believe will indirectly drive activation, such as creating communications that are more strongly branded, funnier, or more attention-getting. Others may be operating under the assumption that as long as they are checking the boxes with efforts in each of the various marketing disciplines—such as maintaining a Facebook page, running programs at retail, launching a loyalty program, and developing branded experiences—they will inherently be activating effectively. Some are likely hindered by organizational comfort or capabilities that are limited to a select group of activities. Many may simply not know what other specialized disciplines could do to help them activate their brands, or may be intimidated by their complexity.

The situation has not been helped by the self-perpetuating nature of the fragmentation of disciplines. Marketers who come from one area or the other will often see marketing challenges through the familiar lens of their expertise—the when-one-has-a-hammer-everything-looks-like-a-nail phenomenon—which propagates a bias or overemphasis, and often even an explicit advocacy for one discipline over the others. The result can be a seductive but dangerous form of oversimplification. Tropes such as "It's all about social," "Everything is retail," and "Content is king," certainly make powerful points about utilizing discipline expertise more broadly, but they also often result in one-discipline-fits-all solutions that fail to acknowledge and take advantage of all of the most efficient and effective opportunities available to activate behavior, to the detriment of ROI.

The marketing technology "flavor of the day" phenomenon is another version of the same challenge. As marketing channels, tactics, and technologies come into favor, there is a strong pull to heavy up in that area that runs counter to a more methodical and disciplined approach to brand activation. From new marketing automation platforms, Pinterest, and Snapchat, to pop-up experiences, stunts, and viral videos, the next new shiny object can disproportionately influence marketers who do not want to be perceived as missing out on the latest trends. This is particularly true in the absence of a construct or rubric for decision making linked directly to the KPIs that drive real business results.

There is also clearly a challenging complexity to managing a growing group of specialties that are evolving and expanding at an increasingly rapid rate driven by the technologies behind them. It is difficult enough for marketers to actually be applying each of the marketing disciplines individually in a best-in-class way, that the challenge of also effectively interconnecting them can seem overwhelming.

For better or worse, however, doing just that is not only the key to more effective activation and improved ROI, but it is also critical to seamlessly engaging today's cross-channel consumers who expect relevant communications and a unified experience regardless of touchpoint as they move fluidly across them. That is the purpose behind utilizing an approach such as the AIM, which places at its center the consumer and the unique path each takes on their journey toward transaction, and aligns the various disciplines into a marketing ecosystem around it. That ecosystem not only embraces each discipline's unique strengths, but also provides a framework for leveraging each one's key best practices to enhance the others.

For those companies that fully embrace the brand- and business-building power of more-effective cross-channel activation, there will ultimately be critical implications for personnel, organizational design, and workflow processes, each of which will need to be strategically addressed.

Most importantly, organizations and their marketing partners will require creative and strategic leadership with real expertise across all of the marketing disciplines and a deep understanding of how to connect them program-matically to their greatest effect. That may be the most formidable challenge for organizations to overcome, given the fragmented state of the industry as a whole and, as a result, the limited number of practitioners credibly expert in operating at a sophisticated level across the full breadth of the marketing landscape.

Once identified, those strategic and creative leaders will require the spe-cialized support of technology partners capable of the development and implementation of the systems and platforms behind their solutions; a robust data science practice proficient at managing large data sets and predictively modeling potential outcomes; and a professionalized project management function capable of managing a truly interconnected, cross-channel develop-ment process.

Establishing those strategies, structures, processes, and people is the criti-cal first step toward institutionalizing more-effective brand activation. They will become the foundation upon which the organization can then build out the teams, partners, and areas of expertise required to execute the intercon-nected mobile, social, retail, experiential, and database marketing efforts that will fully activate their brands to greatest effect. It is a mission that must be undertaken thoughtfully and with the support of key organizational leaders and partners who not only understand the vision, but who also can assess the relative strengths and weaknesses of the potential strategies, structures, processes, and people required.

This foundational work will pay measurable dividends going forward, in the form of more-effective and -efficient marketing programs that better connect with the way today's consumers live, shop, and buy. As will quickly become apparent, however, these efforts will not be optional. Instead, they will ultimately become critical to the success of virtually every marketing or-ganization, brand, and program. These changes will not only be driven by the influx of newly available marketing technologies, effectiveness data, and ROI pressures, but also by the rise of mobile and the expectations of consumers with an increasing capability to bypass marketing communications entirely, along with the brands that cannot keep up with their evolving needs and expectations.

This reality, and the limited talent pool to address it, should and will quickly get the attention of all modern marketing organizations as they recognize that all of the data and technology capabilities in the world will be at best subop-timal, and at worst ineffective, without true cross-channel, cross-discipline thinkers who can effectively utilize them strategically and creatively in-market. As a result, moving quickly to at least begin identifying key leaders from within and outside of an organization to advance these efforts will provide early adopters with a substantial competitive edge in the near and mid-term that will be difficult for late entries to erase. The war for talent that has most re-cently been focused on identifying and securing leading players in digital and data science will quickly shift to those with true cross-discipline expertise, and that universe of potential talent is substantially smaller, inevitably increasing scarcity and costs for those not moving quickly.

Prior or parallel to the type of robust strategic implementation efforts discussed above, organizations can, however, begin to take advantage of the power of the AIM with their existing personnel and partners, and we would strongly encourage them to do so. Once an organization begins to experience the measurable improvements in marketing performance that the AIM can enable even under less-than-optimal conditions, its momentum and incen-tives to make the required changes will only increase.

AIM FOR RESULTS

Brand activation is about driving measurable behavior change, and as a result, the AIM to achieve it is designed to be put into practice. Nothing speaks louder to an organization than real-world results, which is why we encourage each reader to take the AIM for a test drive for themselves by implementing its ap-proach on a select marketing challenge and measuring the in-market impact.

Simply identify an upcoming marketing opportunity, time frame, and budget that is analogous to the organization's recent marketing efforts. Those previous efforts will provide a baseline for comparison when the similar time frame and budget is implemented utilizing the AIM. If the reader's organiza-tion has a history of doing holiday, summer, or other annual programs, for example, select one and consider the typical budget and results from such efforts as the baseline. As outlined in chapter 2, make sure all of the KPIs are clearly defined, linked to real business drivers, and quantifiable via measure-ment plans already in place.

To provide a solid basis for comparison, utilize the same defined target from the baseline efforts, as well as the same brand foundations and guide-

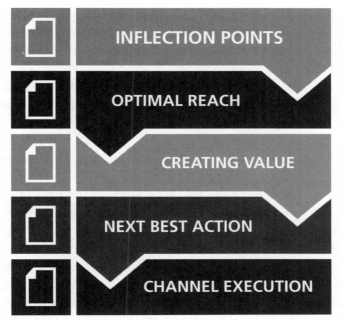

FIGURE 12.1
Strategic and creative briefs cascade from understanding the shopper's journey.
Source: Designed by Sarah Vonderhaar.

lines if possible. Identifying the appropriate, high-value "who" against which to target brand-activation efforts is critical pre-work for optimal application of the AIM, as is a clear understanding of the brand and its opportunities to resonate with that target, but to deviate from the approaches to both taken in the base case would fail to isolate variables and the true impact of employing the AIM in this initial application.

MOMENTS THAT MATTER

The first task for any organization interested in applying the AIM to improve brand activation is to identify the optimal moments to engage with the target consumer, shopper, or prospect to overcome barriers or accelerate movement toward the desired purchase behavior. The more precisely the desired business results have been identified, the more precisely the associated behaviors can be identified as well.

As discussed earlier in chapters 2 and 4, the best way to do this is by analyzing the path-to-purchase from the point of transaction backwards, identifying near misses, and the barriers and opportunities to drive more individuals more quickly toward the ultimate goal of a purchase.

This initial brief should be given to the individuals in the organization and/ or partners who best understand the target audience's most likely journey(s). This may be the organization's sales teams, shopper or retail marketing teams, or their partners, and their answers to the brief could be based on existing data, new qualitiative or quantiative research, or simply their experience and intuition.

Their goal should be to identify precisely where along the prime targets' paths-to-purchase the organization has the biggest opportunity to impact their movement toward transaction. Are not enough people aware of the brand or product, leading to an upper-funnel opportunity to send more prospects on the journey? Is the organization losing too many prospects to competitors with perceived superior features or benefits midway through the shopping journey? Or are brand intenders being stolen at the last moment by the competition at the physical or digital point of purchase, pointing to a lower-funnel area of opportunity?

The team should identify all of the moments of greatest opportunity and place them in rank order, as, depending on budget, the organization may have the ability to address one or several.

The results of this initial brief and exercise will drive the inputs for the next cascading brief, which is to determine how to best address these identified priority moments.

AIM TO REACH

If the outputs of the initial path-to-purchase analysis identified the key behavior moments that matter, the next task is to determine how to best reach the consumers, shoppers, or prospects at those moments to engage them and drive behavior change.

Understanding those moments, when and where they occur, and the target individuals' thoughts and feelings during them will enable the organization to identify the best channels to utilize to reach those individuals.

As discussed in chapters 2 and 5, digital and mobile marketing platforms and tactics offer tremendous opportunities to seamlessly interact with consumers, shoppers, and prospects in the moments that matter most, but there are myriad other potential channels to explore, consider, and evaluate as well. Retail opportunities from brick-and-mortar to e-commerce and e-tail (chapter 4), experiential programs and events (chapter 9), content marketing efforts (chapter 6), and sponsorships (chapter 8) are just a few, and many of them may be strategically utilized in combination. As a result, this second brief should be issued to the individuals in the organization and/or the partners with the best grasp of all potential media channels, and in particular the ability to utilize digital and mobile platforms in a best-in-class way to reach the target consumer/shopper/prospect. This may be a media leader and/or media partner working in combination with a digital leader and/or partner to recommend the optimal channels of engagement for each identified inflection point.

Additionally, this second brief should include the task of identifying the data-capture opportunities within each recommended engagement channel, as these will be critical in delivering the optimal messages and content to each individual or segment moving forward, as discussed in chapter 7.

AIM FOR VALUE

With the key moments and appropriate communications channels identified, those conclusions can inform the third cascading brief, which will focus on how to create sufficient value or incentive for the consumer, shopper, or prospect to be willing to engage at those critical points of contact.

As we discussed extensively in chapters 2, 6, and 8, creating true engagement with individuals requires creating sufficient value to warrant an interaction, and techniques from engagement, experiential, and content marketing can be particularly helpful in achieving it. This brief should be delivered to the person within the organization or among its partners who has the most expertise in creating programs that drive engagement and participation. This may be a direct marketing leader/partner, a retail marketing leader/partner, an experiential and/or promotion marketing leader/partner, or a combination of each.

This brief should also include select creative leaders with strong conceptual abilities, as the outputs of this brief will be program ideas with tactics and themes that drive true participation and involvement.

The outputs of this brief could include cause-related programs; games, contests, or sweepstakes; access to branded experiences; sampling events; content programs; added-value offers of utility, personalization, or customization; stunts; or sports and entertainment sponsorships. Wherever possible, look for opportunities to match the engagement offer with the needs and wants of the recipient for maximum effect.

One of the key criteria of success for this set of deliverables needs to be the conceptual development of programs, offers, and incentives that are inherently linked to the brand. The goal here cannot be engagement for engagement's sake, but must, instead, be engagement that delivers value to the consumer/shopper/prospect in a way that clearly reinforces key differentiated aspects of the brand, as was discussed in chapters 2 and 8. One of the most effective ways to interrogate engagement ideas for their brand-building power is to imagine the program without any brand-identifying imagery—from typography and color to logos and imagery—and assess if without those cues the program could possibly be attributed to a competitor. Ideally the tactic itself and the way it creates value for the recipient should be uniquely tied to the brand so as to be unmistakably associated with it, even in the absence of identifying logos or visual branding.

AIM FOR THE NEXT BEST ACTION

The next and final brief to cascade from the previous brief's outputs is to determine how to identify and deliver the right content, message, or offer to the target audience following their initial engagement to best move them closer toward transaction.

Determining the optimal content moving forward can leverage the next-best-action approach from the worlds of database marketing and CRM, as discussed in chapter 7. At this stage, the brief is to determine how to best sequence the communications going forward based on insights into the targets' most likely potential barriers, objections, or off-ramps on their journey toward transaction, as well as potential needs, desires, or other opportunities to accelerate that journey.

There will inevitably be a finite number of likely paths that key prospect segments will take moving forward, and an equally definable universe of potential barriers or accelerators. Based on those, this brief should focus on identifying the right messages to address each path, barrier, and opportunity by target. Potential barriers could include a target's perceptions that the brand's products are too expensive, "not right for me," or not worth the risk of switching, each of which can lend itself to a different stream of communications, offers, or incentives designed to address them. Potential accelerators

SAMPLE MASTER BRIEF

PRODUCT/BRAND:

PROJECT:

KPI(S):

AUDIENCE
- Target (Brand User and Shopper; could be same):
- Relationship to Brand:
- Relationship to Category:

BRAND
- Purpose:
- Essence/Promise:
- Personality (Voice, Tone, Behaviors):
- Values:
- Key Equities/Assets:

CURRENT FRAME
- Key Competitors:
- Category Dynamics:
- Business Challenge:
- Behavioral Challenge:

INFLECTION POINTS
- Shopper Missions/Journeys (By target):
- Key Inflection Points (Obstacles and opportunities, by journey):
- Behavioral Objective (By inflection point):

OPTIMAL REACH
- Opportunities for Engagement (By inflection point):
- Relevant Channels for Engagement (By inflection point):
- Key Content/Messaging (By inflection point):

CREATING VALUE
- Target Needs & Desires (By inflection point):
- Relevant Brand Assets/Content:

NEXT BEST ACTION
- Next Potential Barrier/Opportunity (By target):
- Relevant Content/Messages (By target):
- Optimal Messaging Sequence (By target):

CHANNEL EXECUTION
- Required Elements:
- Targeted Versions:
- Creative/Executional Mandatories:

FIGURE 12.2

All briefs need to be customized to the brand.

Source: Designed by Sarah Vonderhaar.

might include the target's belief that "I won't get this opportunity again," "This gives me a competitive edge," or "My kids will love it."

When marketing communications are viewed as part of a complete eco-system, it becomes clear that the initial point of contact or engagement is most powerfully viewed as an initial opportunity to demonstrate sufficient value in order to earn the right to continue to engage and provide value. As a result, it is the subsequent series of communications and content that will need to do the heavy lifting of activating target behaviors, meaning, it is critical that they are targeted to overcome the most likely obstacles and seize the most likely opportunities. Even ensuring that just the highest-value segment's communication needs are addressed will result in a no-table increase in effectiveness; and if a select number of other top prospects are also targeted, all the better. While the end game will be to achieve true mass micro-personalization—so that the brand is able to identify, segment, and deliver individualized content to align with each prospect's unique path-to-purchase—simply aligning messaging with top prospects will generate sufficient improvement in results as to build organizational momentum for the efforts and validate the power of strategically aligning disciplines and content via the AIM.

AIM FOR BETTER EXECUTION

With the cascading series of briefs complete and answered, it is now time to brief each of the organization's discipline leaders and/or specialist partners to begin executing the creative assets required for each channel. Each group should understand the program idea, theme, expression, and communication task that each element they are creating needs to achieve. One leader or partner should be assigned the overarching oversight of the execution phase, to ensure that the intent of the original briefs and communications architecture is pre-served and that the program hangs together both strategically and creatively.

The actual in-market performance of the program should be carefully tracked according to the preestablished measurement plan and the results compared to the selected base programs. We invite those who do to share their outcomes with us at activationimperative.com.

When this type of methodical and disciplined approach to brand activation is employed, the program, market impact, and results can be as impressive as Kimberly-Clark's recent efforts on behalf of their iconic brand, Kleenex.

A CASE IN POINT

At the outset of 2015, Kleenex was leading a category that was in severe decline. For nearly fifteen years, Kleenex, along with the other players in the category, had been seeing consistent year-over-year sales declines of 16%, resulting in nearly $500 million of lost revenue for Kleenex alone. The reason: More and more consumers saw no purpose for tissues beyond wiping their noses when they were ill, and for that they believed they could use toilet paper, generic tissues, or paper towels. Even Kleenex's most loyal consumers—moms who kept a box of tissues in every room of the house—were choosing store brands. They simply did not see the value in paying more for a premium tissue when a cheaper alternative would do.

The brand needed to overcome consumers' perceptions that it was only useful when they were sick *and* needed to demonstrate its value over store brands. In short, Kleenex needed to be something more than just paper in a "sick box."

Kleenex's marketing leadership aligned on the goals of changing brand perceptions while growing Kleenex's business, and ultimately tracked three interrelated objectives and corresponding performance benchmarks for the brand's 2015 marketing effort:

Business objective: Grow category share and Kleenex brand sales. Increasing category share and sales were essential to driving Kleenex's bottom line.

KPI: Grow Kleenex sales by +0.6% while growing category share +0.3 points versus the previous year.

Behavioral objective: Increase social engagement with the Kleenex brand. This would demonstrate that the new message was resonating and advancing consumers along their paths-to-purchase.

KPI: Increase engagement with the brand by 15% versus the previous year.

Perceptual objective: Increase the emotional resonance of the Kleenex brand. In order to achieve the brand's full potential, Kleenex needed to be thought of not just as a tool for wiping a runny nose, but as something more meaningful and relevant anytime, not just during cold and flu season.

KPI: Increase emotional resonance of Kleenex by 5% versus the previous year (measured by independent third-party research).

To accomplish these ambitious objectives, the brand needed to rally its most loyal fans while also building its next generation of consumers.

Loyal moms, who had grown up with Kleenex, but were beginning to question the brand's value compared with lower-cost options, clearly needed to be won back. Millennials, however, who had little emotional connection to tissues brands or products, and did not see them playing a role in their lives, had to be won over or the category would essentially disappear in a matter of years. As the most altruistic generation to date, Millennials choose brands based on alignment with their values, so Kleenex needed to communicate that it stands for an idea they could relate to.

With these two high-value targets identified, the question became where they should best be reached along their respective paths-to-purchase, and what types of communications would engage them. In the case of Millennials, who largely remained out of the category, the key inflection point was at the very top of the funnel, with the opportunity to begin them down a path-to-purchase. With moms, the key inflection points were closer to the point of transaction, pre-shopping when they developed their list and at retail, both points where they often opted for store brands. But in a category full of functional benefit communications, how could Kleenex stand out?

When everyone in the category is proclaiming "soft and strong," there is no good reason to choose one brand over the other. Making matters worse, most of the advertising depicts sneezing sufferers reaching for a tissue, reinforcing the category's association with sickness. Not only is the negative connotation a problem, but when shoppers only purchase Kleenex during flu season, the brand misses out on months' worth of sales. Clearly, talking about function was not going to cut it anymore. Kleenex needed to reach consumers through a more emotional and broadly relevant message.

Qualitative and quantitative research conducted by the brand's marketing team uncovered a universal truth that connected both target audiences: Each puts a disproportionately high value on empathy—on showing care through a human connection.

The brand also learned that 50% of people in the United States say they have "missed an opportunity to show someone they cared."[1] In an age of ubiquitous mobile devices, staring at a cell phone is unfortunately easier than acknowledging each other's needs—and this fact bothered moms in particular. In-home depth interviews[2] revealed that moms actively worried about whether their children would develop enough empathy growing up in an online world.

These insights led to Kleenex's big idea: People—and Kleenex's target audiences in particular—*want* to show they care, and Kleenex had an opportunity to fill the gap. In an apathetic world, Kleenex could be that human connection. Kleenex could stand for empathy and help people fight indifference through a simple gesture of care.

As a result of this research, Kleenex saw an opportunity to reposition the brand from a cold-and-flu wipe to an everyday gesture of care. This new strategy would become the key to keeping Kleenex alive and healthy, and to creating content and experiences that the Kleenex targets would value and engage with. It was also authentic to the brand, as caring and empathy had been part of Kleenex's ethos all along; they just needed to be revealed and revitalized.

The ensuing 2015 marketing program brought Kleenex to life as a simple and universal gesture of care by sharing authentic moments when empathy triumphed over indifference. The tagline—"Kleenex. Someone needs one"—became the universal truth that launched a breakthrough cross-channel program that included an innovative take on out-of-home advertising and a pioneering partnership with Facebook.

The unique, out-of-home "Careboard"—a custom, first-of-its-kind billboard made up of real, ready-to-use Kleenex boxes—was a key element of the

FIGURE 12.3
The unique, out-of-home "Careboard"—a custom, first-of-its-kind billboard made up of real, ready-to-use Kleenex boxes.
Source: Kimberly-Clark.

program. Spelling out encouraging messages of support using actual tissues allowed Kleenex to physically deliver the product and brand at real, life-changing moments. To extend these experiential efforts online, the program also offered an interactive online experience that allowed consumers everywhere to create their own messages of care on virtual Careboards and post these messages to their social networks. If a user shared a message with a friend, the user would receive a higher-value coupon. If that friend shared her own message, she would receive the transaction-driving reward as well—creating a progression of both feel-good messages and incentives to purchase the brand at retail.

The brand toured the country, creating and filming authentic, inspiring, culturally relevant moments of care—some featuring the Careboard—and shared these moments through a groundbreaking social media effort that connected with consumers at a more emotional level. Kleenex partnered with Facebook to deliver video stories of care to viewers at the most timely and relevant moments—such as to a new mom up late at night, or to a woman newly engaged—truly delivering the right content to the right person at the right time. One of the videos, about Chance, a disabled dog, and his disabled owner, touched viewers so deeply that it moved them to share at unprecedented levels, racking up more than sixty million views to date. To drive purchase, a targeted banner ad then led viewers to the Kleenex website for a special retail offer.

Broadcast television reinforced the big idea on a larger scale. The films were the megaphone for spreading the idea that "Someone needs one" through heartwarming commercials that showed often-overlooked everyday moments of care designed to inspire people to act instead of remaining indifferent to the world around them. The television commercials were targeted at Kleenex consumers and placed in contextual programming more likely to drive an emotional response.

Social media was also vital, given Kleenex's desire to make care contagious. It is not surprising, then, that the channel strategy focused on the places easiest for women to connect and share with others: their social networks. These channels were not only where Kleenex's targets spend the most time online, but also the places where they could (and wanted) to share. Retargeting via Facebook then helped close the sale, as those who were exposed to the custom content were retargeted to provide them with a valuable incentive to purchase.

In addition to contextual and behavioral targeting in digital media, paid search also capitalized on the heightened awareness and energy surrounding the campaign through both search engine and paid YouTube support. You-Tube was specifically used to expand the custom content beyond Facebook, targeted to women who were interested in emotionally compelling, care-infused categories like romance and drama films, dating services, and gift cards and greetings.

Special packages at retail enabled consumers to write their own custom messages of care on their Kleenex packs, linking the in-aisle and at-home experience to the digital, social, experiential, and broadcast messaging.

The results tell the story:

Business objective: Grow category share and Kleenex brand sales.

Result: Actual sales increased 4.5× vs. expectations (+2.7% vs. 2014), accounting for a 5.7× share gain vs. expectations (+1.7pts vs. 2014).[3]

Behavioral objective: Increase social engagement with Kleenex brand.

Result: The first eleven weeks of the 2015 program (6/8–8/21) led to 44× social engagements (shares, comments, likes, and clicks) vs. all of 2014.[4]

Perceptual objective: Increase emotional perception of Kleenex brand.

Result: "Kleenex provides me a way to show others that I care" and "Kleenex provides emotional comfort" were the top messages taken away from the 2015 program, with an 8.5% and 103% increase, respectively, from the previous year.[5]

A clear, ownable, relevant, value-creating brand and content idea—that we live in an indifferent world, and Kleenex can help us fight that indifference—combined with data-based insights and innovative approaches that bridged digital, social, and experiential to reach high-value targets at the right time with the right message all worked in concert to create the kind of results any marketer would be proud of. The fact that the category continued its more than decade-long sales decline while Kleenex posted a year-over-year sales gain makes the result all the more impressive and the approach even more worthy of note.

The industry took notice and awarded this innovative, cross-channel program an Effie, the marketing world's most prestigious prize for effectiveness, in recognition of its exceptional results building both the Kleenex brand and its business. By focusing on clearly defined and measurable objectives, and taking a human-centered, behavioral approach to addressing them, Kleenex demonstrated the power of a strategically and creatively coordinated approach to brand activation that maximized effectiveness and created value for participant and marketer alike.

OUR ACTIVATION IMPERATIVE

Today's marketers have an unprecedented set of tools with which to build their brands and business. The days of considering those goals as oppositional are long past, and the rewards for those who embrace a coordinated approach to both are great.

With new technologies, platforms, and information available almost daily, the task is clearly not a small one, and the challenges far from simple. Rising to the occasion, however, is clearly not as much a choice as it is a mandate for any marketing organization interested in engaging today's consumers as they would like to be engaged and maximizing the value of their efforts to their enterprise and its patrons.

The Activation Imperative and its method were created to provide today's marketers a path forward that would not just create synergies among their disparate marketing efforts, but would also utilize each to its full effect individually, as well as to amplify the others. The goal was a construct for decision making that would transcend current trends and the appearance or disappearance of new technologies, platforms, and channels, to consistently enable a more modern and measurably effective approach to the development of marketing plans, strategies, tactics, and creative.

The shift from simply building brands to fully activating them is on, driven by demands for greater marketing return from brands and expectations of greater value from consumers. The time has come to not simply shift the conversation, but also our approaches and actions, to recognize and unlock the full power of a diverse marketing landscape to activate brands, activate consumers, and ultimately, activate behaviors.

That is both the challenge and the opportunity of the activation imperative. Now, let's get started.

Notes

CHAPTER 1

1. Michael A. Stelzner, "2014 Social Media Marketing Industry Report," *Social Media Examiner* (www.socialmediaexaminer.com/SocialMediaMarketingIndustryReport2014.pdf), accessed July 19, 2015.

2. Michael Becker, "Using Big Data to Learn Consumer Habits," *Relevance* (relevance.com/using-big-data-to-learn-consumer-habits/), accessed July 19, 2015.

3. Micah Solomon, "2015 Is the Year of the Millennial Customer: 5 Key Traits These 80 Million Consumers Share," *Forbes* (www.forbes.com/sites/micahsolomon/2014/12/29/5-traits-that-define-the-80-million-millennial-customers-coming-your-way/), accessed July 19, 2015.

4. Nigel Hollis, "How Smart Brands Command a Premium Price," Millward Brown (www.millwardbrown.com/Insights/Point-of-View/How_Smart_Brands_Command_a_Premium_Price/default.aspx), accessed July 1, 2016.

5. Frederick Crawford, "This Is What Companies That Survive the Recession Do Right," *Bloomberg Business* (www.bloomberg.com/bw/articles/2014-08-29/the-companies-that-can-survive-recession-do-these-things-right), accessed July 20, 2015.

6. Panos Mourdoukoutas, "Apple's Most Important Branding Lesson for Marketers," *Forbes* (www.forbes.com/sites/panosmourdoukoutas/2013/10/05/apples-most-important-branding-lesson-for-marketers/), accessed July 20, 2015.

7. Eve Reiter, "How Marketers Can Reduce Tension in Managing Multiple Agency Relationships," *Ad Age* (adage.com/article/guest-columnists/marketers-reducing-tension-multiple-agency-relationships/144550/), accessed July 20, 2015.

8. Rory Sutherland, "Begin at the End to Plan the Consumer Journey," Warc, *Market Leader*, Quarter 2, 2015 (warc.com), accessed June 16, 2015.

9. Sutherland, "Begin at the End to Plan the Consumer Journey."

10. "2011 Silver Winner—Walgreens—Arm Yourself for the Ones You Love" (www.youtube.com/watch?v=51SKsJ21G_w), accessed June 15, 2016.

11. "Arm Yourself for the Ones You Love," Chief Marketer (www.chiefmarketer.com/arm-yourself-for-the-ones-you-love/), accessed June 15, 2016.

12. "IKEA 3D Cover" (www.youtube.com/watch?v=HPl9ZqvXEFg), accessed June 15, 2016.

13. "Running Products," Nike (www.nike.com/us/en_us/c/running/), accessed July 1, 2016.

14. Jim Tanous, "A History of the Apple Back to School Promotion," *Tek Revue* (www.tekrevue.com/apple-back-to-school-history/), accessed July 20, 2015.

15. Jim Rossignol, "Apple Launched Back to School Promotion, Offers a Free Beats Solo2 Headphone with Mac Purchase," *MacRumors* (www.macrumors .com/2015/07/23/back-to-school-promo-beats-2015/), accessed August 5, 2015.

16. Laura Northrup, "Best Buy Might Give You a Free iPod If You Know to Ask," *Consumerist* (consumerist.com/2010/06/02/best-buy-will-match-apples-free-ipod-promotion-but-only-if-you-know-to-ask/), accessed July 1, 2016.

17. Greg Hernandez and Greg Johnson, "Taco Bell Replaces Chief, Chihuahua as Sales Fall," *LA Times* (articles.latimes.com/2000/jul/19/business/fi-55188), accessed July 5, 2016.

18. Rose DeWolf, "Those Creative TV Ads Can Be a Commercial Failure," *Inquirer Daily News* (articles.philly.com/1997-11-25/news/25542942_1_tv-ads-new-ad-agency-duracell), accessed July 6, 2016.

19. "Can Repeating a Brand Claim Lead to Memory Confusion?," *Journal of Marketing Research* 39, no. 3 (August 2002) (www.jstor.org/stable/1558600?seq=1#page_scan_tab_contents).

20. Adam Ferrier, with Jennifer Fleming, *The Advertising Effect: How to Change Behavior* (South Melbourne, Victoria, Australia: Oxford University Press, 2014).

21. Jason DeMers, "How to Use the AIDA Formula to Boost Content Marketing Strategy," *Forbes* (www.forbes.com/sites/jaysondemers/2013/08/05/how-to-use-the-aida-formula-to-boost-your-content-marketing-strategy/), accessed July 1, 2016.

22. Annmarie Hanlon, "The AIDA Model," Smart Insights (www.smartinsights.com/traffic-building-strategy/offer-and-message-development/aida-model/), accessed July 6, 2016.

23. "A 4-Step Writing Formula for Ad Agency New Business," *Fuel Lines* (www.fuelingnewbusiness.com/2013/02/27/use-the-aida-formula-to-simplify-your-content-marketing/), accessed July 2016.

24. Ferrier, with Fleming, *The Advertising Effect*, 5.

25. Ferrier, with Fleming, *The Advertising Effect*, 6.

26. Ferrier, with Fleming, *The Advertising Effect*, 41.

27. "The Death of Mega Brands, Part 1" (www.forbes.com/sites/robinlewis/2013/12/19/the-death-of-mega-brands-part-1/).

28. "Twilight of the Brands," *New Yorker* (www.newyorker.com/magazine/2014/02/17/twilight-brands).

29. "The Decline of Brands," *Wired* (archive.wired.com/wired/archive/12.11/brands.html).

30. "Brands Aren't Dead, but Traditional Branding Tools Are Dying," *Harvard Business Review* (hbr.org/2014/02/the-brand-is-dead-long-live-the-brand/).

CHAPTER 2

1. Coca-Cola (www.shareacoke.com/#personalized), accessed August 14, 2015.

2. Coca-Cola (name.shareacoke.com/), accessed August 14, 2015.

3. "Bill Backer Interviewed About 'I'd Like to Buy the World a Coke' " (www.youtube.com/watch?v=tSNU1TvF4pc), accessed August 14, 2015.

4. "Pepsi Advertising," American Art Archives (www.americanartarchives.com/pepsi.htm), accessed August 14, 2015.

5. Malloy Russell, "OOPS: Pepsi Let Trademark Lapse On 'Choice of a New Generation'—Now It's Owned by an Oatmeal Company," *Business Insider* (www .businessinsider.com/better-oats-uses-pepsis-tagline-in-new-campaign-2012-3), accessed August 14, 2015.

6. "Pepsi Generation" (en.wikipedia.org/wiki/Pepsi_Generation), accessed August 14, 2015.

7. Craig Bida, "Why Pepsi Canned the Refresh Project," *MediaPost* (www .mediapost.com/publications/article/186127/why-pepsi-canned-the-refresh-project .html), accessed August 15, 2015.

8. Natalie Zmuda, "Pepsi Tackles Identity Crisis," *Advertising Age* (adage.com/ article/news/pepsi-tackles-identity-crisis/234586/), accessed August 15, 2015.

9. Zmuda, "Pepsi Tackles Identity Crisis."

10. Lara O'Reilly, "Pepsi Is Taking an Audacious Swipe at Coke's Polar Bears," *Business Insider* (www.businessinsider.com/pepsi-ad-pokes-fun-at-share-a-coke-and-coca-colas-polar-bears-2015-6), accessed August 14, 2015.

11. "WWF and the Coca-Cola Company Team Up to Protect Polar Bears," World Wildlife Fund (www.worldwildlife.org/projects/wwf-and-the-coca-cola-company-team-up-to-protect-polar-bears), accessed August 14, 2015.

12. "Renewing Our Partnership, Expanding Our Impact," *Coca-Cola Journey* (www .coca-colacompany.com/stories/converging-on-water-an-innovative-conservation-partnership), accessed August 14, 2015.

13. "Coke Raises More Than $2 Million to Save Polar Bears," *Coca-Cola Journey* (www.coca-colacompany.com/our-company/coke-raises-over-2-million-to-save-polar-bears), accessed August 14, 2015.

14. "Mission, Vision, & Values," *Coca-Cola Journey* (www.coca-colacompany.com/ our-company/mission-vision-values), accessed August 14, 2015.

CHAPTER 3

1. Laurence Minsky, *How to Succeed in Advertising When All You Have Is Talent*, 2nd ed. (Chicago: Copy Workshop, 2007).

2. Artie Bulgrin, *ESPN on Cross-Platform Audience Measurement*, a Warc webinar, July 15, 2015.

3. "US Adults Spend 5.5 Hours with Video Content Each Day: Digital Video Viewing Adds Significant Time to the Average US Consumer's Media Day," *Emarketer* (www.emarketer.com/Article/US-Adults-Spend-55-Hours-with-Video-Content-Each-Day/1012362), accessed August 13, 2015.

4. Jacob Margolis, "Company's Secret Weapon to Make Videos Go Viral," *Weekend Edition Saturday* (www.npr.org/2015/04/18/400573717/companys-secret-weapon-to-make-videos-go-viral?sc=tw), accessed August 3, 2015.

5. Stacy Epstein, "Why the Traditional Ad Agency Is a Dying Breed," Mashable (mashable.com/2015/07/30/the-ad-agency-is-dead/), accessed August 3, 2015.

6. Mars Incorporated, "SNICKERS® Teases a 'Very Brady' Super Bowl XLIX Commercial," *PR Newswire* (www.prnewswire.com/news-releases/snickers-teases-a-very-brady-super-bowl-xlix-commercial-300023525.html), accessed July 4, 2016.

7. "You're Not You When You're Hungry," 2011 Gold Effie Winner, Effie Awards (current.effie.org/downloads/2011_5627_pdf_1.pdf), accessed August 3, 2015.

8. Sarah Begley, "The 13 Most Influential Candy Bars of All Time," *Time* (newsfeed.time.com/2014/02/18/13-most-influential-candy-bars-of-all-time/slide/snickers/), accessed July 4, 2016.

9. "You Can't Wait to Get It On," Bronze Effie Winner, Effie Awards (effie.org/case_studies/case/2010), accessed August 3, 2015.

10. Minsky, *How to Succeed in Advertising When All You Have Is Talent.*

11. Barry Schwartz, *The Paradox of Choice: Why More Is Less* (New York: Harper Perennial, 2004).

12. S. H. Kazmi and Satish K. Batra, *Advertising & Sale Promotion*, 3rd ed. (New Delhi: Excel Books, 2008), 145.

13. George A. Akerlof and William T. Dickens, "The Economic Consequences of Cognitive Dissonance," *Explorations in Pragmatic Economics: Selected Papers of George A. Akerlof and Coauthors* (Oxford: Oxford University Press, 2005), 190.

14. David Aron, "The Effect of Counter-Experiential Marketing Communication on Satisfaction and Repurchase Intention," *Journal of Consumer Satisfaction, Dissatisfaction, and Complaining Behavior*, 19, January 1, 2006.

15. Minsky, *How to Succeed in Advertising When All You Have Is Talent.*

16. Jeanine Poggi, "The Next Phase of Addressable Advertising: Understanding TV ROI," *Ad Age* (adage.com/article/dataworks/phase-addressable-advertising-understanding-tv-roi/295550/), accessed August 3, 2015.

17. Jeanine Poggi, "The CMO's Guide to Addressable TV Advertising: The Comcast-Time Warner Cable Combination Could Speed Things Up," *Ad Age* (adage.com/article/cmo-strategy/cmo-s-guide-addressable-tv-advertising/291728/), accessed July 4, 2016.

18. www.dishmediasales.com/addressable/, accessed August 21, 2015.

19. Kashmir Hill, "How Target Figured Out a Teen Girl Was Pregnant Before Her Father Did," *Forbes* (www.forbes.com/sites/kashmirhill/2012/02/16/how-target-figured-out-a-teen-girl-was-pregnant-before-her-father-did/), accessed July 4, 2016.

20. Charles Duhigg, "How Companies Learn Your Secrets," *New York Times Magazine* (www.nytimes.com/2012/02/19/magazine/shopping-habits.html?pagewanted=1&_r=3&hp&), accessed July 4, 2016.

21. Diane Williams, "The Arbitron National In-Car Study, 2009 Edition," Arbitron (www.arbitron.com/downloads/InCarStudy2009.pdf), accessed July 4, 2016.

22. Nielsen, "State of the Media: Audio Today (How America Listens)," (www.nielsen.com/us/en/insights/reports/2015/state-of-the-media-audio-today-how-america-listens.html), accessed July 4, 2016.

23. Nielsen, "State of the Art."

24. Nielsen, "State of the Art."

25. Neal Rubin, "The Death of Radio: Is It Time to Plan the Wake?," *Detroit News* (www.detroitnews.com/story/opinion/columnists/neal-rubin/2014/12/04/radio-dying/19867701/), accessed July 4, 2016.

26. Pew Research Center, State of the News Media 2015, "Newspapers: Circulation by Publication Type," (www.journalism.org/media-indicators/newspaper-circulation/), accessed August 19, 2015.

27. Guy Consterdine, "Proof of Performance: Making the Case for Magazine Media, Volume 2," *FIPP Insight* (www.fipp.com/insight/toolkit/pop-toolkit), accessed August 3, 2015.

28. USA TouchPoints, 2014.1: OOH and Today's Mobile Consumer, RealityMite for the Outdoor Advertising Association of America, 2015.

29. Williams, "The Arbitron National In-Car Study, 2009 Edition." One caveat: The report noted that the "2003 study was fielded during the summer and the 2009 study was conducted in winter," which means that Americans might be spending even more time going from one place to the next.

30. Lisa Smith, "The Single Most Important Thing in a Media Buy," *SpokeN: The Spoke 8 Marketing Blog* (go.spoke8marketing.com/blog-1/bid/376872/The-Single-Most-Important-Thing-in-a-Media-Buy), accessed July 4, 2016.

31. Gerald J. Tellis, "Generalizations about Advertising Effectiveness in Markets," *Journal of Advertising Research* 49, no. 2 (June 2009).

32. Gerald J. Tellis, *Effective Advertising: Understanding When, How, and Why Advertising Works* (Thousand Oaks, CA: Sage, 2004), 78–79.

33. "Why, When, and How Much to Entertain Consumers in Advertisements?," *Marketing Science* (pubsonline.informs.org/doi/abs/10.1287/mksc.2014.0854?journal Code=mksc).

34. Tellis, "Generalizations about Advertising Effectiveness in Markets."

35. David Aaker, *Aaker on Branding: 20 Principles That Drive Success* (New York: Morgan James Publishing, 2014).

CHAPTER 4

1. P&G Best of Beauty 2014, Multi-Retailer Program / North America, Effie Awards (effie.org/case_studies/case/SME_2015_9339), accessed July 4, 2016.

2. Independent from us, Ogilvy UK vice chairman Rory Sutherland came to the same advice for a different reason. Visualise Shopper Marketing Conference—2012, Rory Sutherland (www.youtube.com/watch?v=uTz2__bLzs0), accessed August 12, 2015.

3. A. G. Lafley and Ram Charan, *The Game-Changer: How You Can Drive Revenue and Profit Growth with Innovation* (New York: Crown Business, 2008), 5.

4. Emily Nelson and Sarah Ellison, "In a Shift, Marketers Beef Up Ad Spending Inside Stores: Funky Displays and Lighting, TV Spots in Wal-Mart; Unsettling Madison Avenue," *Wall Street Journal* (www.wsj.com/articles/SB112725891535046751), accessed July 4, 2016.

5. Christopher Heine, "By Watching How Customers Shop in the Store, Crate & Barrel Lifts Web Sales 44%: The E-commerce, Brick-and-Mortar Link," *Adweek*

(www.adweek.com/news/technology/watching-how-customers-shop-store-crate-barrel-lifts-web-sales-44-164397), accessed August 8, 2015.

6. Natalie Zmuda, "Tropicana Line's Sales Plunge 20% Post-Rebranding," *Ad Age* (adage.com/article/news/tropicana-line-s-sales-plunge-20-post-rebranding/135735/), accessed September 5, 2015.

7. Hilary Milnes, "Why Target Is Betting on In-Store Technology," *Digiday* (digiday.com/brands/target-beacons/), accessed August 14, 2015.

8. "Bronze: Best In-Store Retail Campaign, Effortless Meals at Walmart," *Chief Marketer* (www.chiefmarketer.com/pro-awards-winners/bronze-best-use-shopper-marketing), accessed July 2, 2016.

9. "Coca-Cola and Meals: Collaborating with Partners for Success," American Marketing Association, Jacksonville Chapter (jaxama.org/driving-bottom-line-results-brand-engagement/), accessed July 2, 2016.

10. "Bronze: Best In-Store Retail Campaign, Effortless Meals at Walmart."

11. "Gold: Best In-Store Retail Campaign, Effortless Meals at Walmart," *Chief Marketer* (www.chiefmarketer.com/pro-awards-winners/gold-best-store-retail-campaign), accessed July 2, 2016.

12. "Gold: Best In-Store Retail Campaign, Effortless Meals at Walmart."

13. "Effie Case Study: Kraft Food Hacks, Shopper Marketing Case Study," Path to Purchase Institute (p2pi.org/article/effie-case-study-kraft-food-hacks), accessed September 7, 2015.

CHAPTER 5

1. "Smartphone Penetration Rate," Statista (www.statista.com/statistics/201183/forecast-of-smartphone-penetration-in-the-us), accessed October 2, 2015.

2. Nick Wingfield, "More Retailers at Risk of Amazon 'Showrooming'," *Bits* (bits.blogs.nytimes.com/2013/02/27/more-retailers-at-risk-of-amazon-showrooming/), accessed October 3, 2015.

3. "State of Montana Turns $25,000 Investment into $6.9 Million, REGGIE Awards Case Studies," Association of National Advertisers (www.ana.net/miccontent/show/id/reggie-2015-montana), accessed September 1, 2015.

4. Jordan Kahn, "GE Integrates iBeacons in New LED Lighting Fixtures Rolling Out in Walmart & Other Retailers," 9to5Mac (9to5mac.com/2014/05/29/ge-integrates-

ibeacons-in-new-led-lighting-fixtures-rolling-out-in-walmart-other-retailers/), accessed October 3, 2015.

5. "Enter the Shoe Aisle, Feel Your Phone Buzz with a Personal Deal," *New York Times*, December 31, 2015.

6. Julie A. Ask, "Winning in Your Customers' Mobile Moments," Julie Ask's Blog, Forrester (blogs.forrester.com/julie_ask/14-05-30-winning_in_your_customers_mobile_moments), accessed July 2, 2016.

7. "Win the Moments That Matter," Think with Google (www.thinkwithgoogle.com/intl/en-gb/blog/post/win-the-moments-that-matter/), accessed September 5, 2015.

8. Julie A. Ask and Douglas Roberge, "Create Mobile Moments with Messaging," Forrester Research (www.forrester.com/report/Create+Mobile+Moments+With+Messaging/-/E-RES118423), accessed October 1, 2014.

9. Mike Brinker, Kasey Lobaugh, and Alison Paul, "The Dawn of Mobile Influence," Deloitte Digital (www.downtowndevelopment.com/pdf/2_us_retail_Mobile_Influence.pdf), accessed September 18, 2015.

10. Ask and Roberge, "Create Mobile Moments with Messaging," 14.

11. Ask and Roberge, "Create Mobile Moments with Messaging," 13.

12. "Pew Research Center American Trends Panel Experience Sampling Survey" (www.pewinternet.org/2015/04/01/u-s-smartphone-use-in-2015/pi_2015-04-01_smartphones_21/), accessed September 18, 2015.

13. "2015 EFFIE Award Preview: Project Architeuthis," Center for Digital Democracy (www.democraticmedia.org/content/2015-effie-award-preview-project-architeuthis), accessed October 7, 2015.

14. "McDonald's for #RMHC, REGGIE Awards Case Studies," Association of National Advertisers (www.ana.net/miccontent/show/id/reggie-2015-mcdonalds), accessed July 2, 2016.

15. "Ice Cream Served with a Smile," Unilever (www.unilever.com/brands/brand-stories/ice-cream-served-with-a-smile.html), accessed September 18, 2015.

16. Jonah Berger and Eric Schwartz, "What Products Do People Talk About, and Why? How Product Characteristics and Promotional Giveaways Shape Word-of-Mouth," Marketing Science Institute (www.msi.org/reports/what-products-do-people-talk-about-and-why-how-product-characteristics-and/?login=required), accessed September 18, 2015.

17. Garett Sloane, "Oreo and Ritz Mark First Super Bowl Ads to Be Purchased Programmatically: Regional Mondelez Spots Are Game Changers," *Adweek* (www .adweek.com/news/technology/oreo-and-ritz-mark-first-super-bowl-ads-be-purchased-programmatically-162633), accessed July 2, 2016.

18. Kate Maddox, "Best Practices: How to Tailor Videos to the Customer Journey," *Ad Age* (adage.com/article/btob/practices-tailor-videos-customer-journey/300038/), accessed September 5, 2015.

19. "Tesco Builds Virtual Shops for Korean Commuters," *Telegraph* (www .telegraph.co.uk/technology/mobile-phones/8601147/Tesco-builds-virtual-shops-for-Korean-commuters.html), accessed September 18, 2015.

20. Elisa Montaguti, Scott A. Neslin, and Sara Valentini, "Do Marketing Campaigns Produce Multichannel Buying and More Profitable Customers? A Field Experiment," Marketing Science Institute (www.msi.org/reports/ do-marketing-campaigns-produce-multichannel-buying-and-more-profitable-cust/?login=required), accessed September 18, 2015.

21. "Mobile Will Account for 72% of US Digital Ad Spend by 2019: Consumer usage and better ad formats drive dollars to mobile apps," eMarketer (http:// www.emarketer.com/Article/Mobile-Will-Account-72-of-US-Digital-Ad-Spend-by-2019/1012258), accessed October 11, 2016.

CHAPTER 6

1. "What Is Content Marketing?," Content Marketing Institute (contentmarket inginstitute.com/what-is-content-marketing/), accessed September 6, 2015.

2. "What Is Content Marketing?," Content Marketing Institute.

3. "The Great International Paper Airplane Book," Amazon (www.amazon.com/ Great-International-Paper-Airplane-Book/dp/0671211293).

4. Christine Crandell, "From Customer Interactions to Emotional Engagement: 5 Trends Shaping Marketing," *CustomerThink* (customerthink.com/from-customer-interactions-to-emotional-engagement-5-trends-shaping-marketing/), accessed August 24, 2015.

5. McKinley Marketing Partners, "2015 Marketing Hiring Trends: Optimizing Teams with Both Traditional and Digital Marketing Expertise" (mckinleymarketingpartners.com/site/wp-content/uploads/2014/12/McKinley_ White_Paper1.pdf), accessed September 29, 2015.

6. Ann Handley and Joe Pulizzi, "2015 Benchmarks, Budgets, and Trends—North America," Content Marketing Institute (contentmarketinginstitute.com/wp-content/uploads/2014/10/2015_B2B_Research.pdf), accessed September 29, 2015.

7. Joline McGoldrick, "Digital Advertising at 21: Marketers Get Savvier about Multigenerational Multiscreen Marketing," *Digital and Media Predictions—2015*, Millward Brown (www.millwardbrown.com/DigitalPredictions/2015/download/Millward-Brown_2015-Digital-and-Media-Predictions.pdf), accessed July 2, 2016.

8. "Content Engagement by Generation" (www.frac.tl/research/content-engagement-by-generation), accessed July 2, 2016.

9. McGoldrick, "Digital Advertising at 21."

10. "Kmart Ship My Pants: Case Study," Warc, accessed September 29, 2015.

CHAPTER 7

1. William Rosen, "Meet Today's Analytic Creative," *Ad Age* (adage.com/article/adagestat/meet-today-s-analytic-creative/229581/), accessed October 10, 2015.

2. "Mobile Ad Spend to Top $100 Billion Worldwide in 2016, 51% of Digital Market: US and China will account for nearly 62% of global mobile ad spending next year," eMarketer (http://www.emarketer.com/Article/Mobile-Ad-Spend-Top-100-Billion-Worldwide-2016-51-of-Digital-Market/1012299), accessed October 11, 2016.

3. Personal communication with Patrick Palmer, June 30, 2016.

4. Steve Lohr, "With the TV Business in Upheaval, Targeted Ads Offer Hope," *New York Times* (www.nytimes.com/2015/10/05/business/media/with-the-tv-business-in-upheaval-targeted-ads-offer-hope.html?_r=1), accessed October 9, 2015.

5. Adam Ferrier, with Jennifer Fleming, *The Advertising Effect: How to Change Behavior* (South Melbourne, Victoria, Australia: Oxford University Press, 2014), 81.

6. Ferrier, with Fleming, *The Advertising Effect*, 80.

7. "Hard Sell / Soft Sell Advertising," *Ad Age* (adage.com/article/adage-encyclopedia/hard-sell-soft-sell-advertising/98687/), accessed October 10, 2015.

8. Debra Aho Williamson, "Creating Ads on the Fly—New Opportunities in Programmatic," eMarketer webinar (www.emarketer.com/Webinar/Creating-Ads-on-FlyNew-Opportunities-Programmatic/4000117), accessed October 10, 2015.

9. Jack Neff, "Axe Remakes Story of Romeo 100,000 Times," *Ad Age* (adage.com/ article/see-the-spot/unilever-s-axe-remakes-story-romeo-100-000-times/299888/), accessed October 9, 2015.

CHAPTER 8

1. Tom White, Institute of Practitioners in Advertising, "Lay's Global: How a Great Idea Traveled the World," Entrant, IPA Effectiveness Awards 2014, accessed October 11, 2015.

2. "Jonah Berger Talks About the Science of Word of Mouth" (www.msi.org/ articles/jonah-berger-talks-about-the-science-of-word-of-mouth/), accessed October 10, 2015.

3. "Tourism Queensland—Best Job in the World," Sapient Nitro (www.sapient. com/content/sapientnitro/en-us.html#work/featured/tourism-queensland/best-job-in-the-world/the-ask/the-ask2), accessed October 8, 2015.

4. Michael Johnsen, "America's Biggest Health Fair Is Coming to Walmart," *Retailing Today* (www.retailingtoday.com/article/americas-biggest-health-fair-coming-walmart), accessed October 11, 2015.

5. "Love. Say It with Milk-Bone," Association of National Advertisers (www.ana.net/ miccontent/show/id/reggie-2015-bigheartpetbrands), accessed October 11, 2015.

6. "SNCF: The Most Serious Game Ever," Cannes Creative Lions, Entrant, Creative Effectiveness Lions, accessed October 11, 2015.

CHAPTER 9

1. "Millennials: Fueling the Experience Economy," EventBrite (eventbrite-s3 .s3.amazonaws.com/marketing/Millennials_Research/Gen_PR_Final.pdf), accessed October 16, 2015.

2. "Case Studies: Occasionally Perfect Billboard" (relevent.com/work/heineken/ occasionally-perfect-billboard), accessed October 18, 2015.

3. "Summit Online" (summit.adobe.com/na/?promoid=KQHDR), accessed October 23, 2015.

4. "Love Has No Labels" (www.adforum.com/creative-work/ad/player/34514701), accessed October 19, 2015.

5. "Adidas's Billboard Ads Give Kick to Japanese Pedestrians" (www.wsj.com/ articles/SB106211104114152600), accessed October 24, 2015.

6. "Adidas—Vertical Football/Soccer" (adland.tv/commercials/adidas-vertical-football-soccer-event-billboard-live-2004-japan), accessed October 24, 2015.

7. Robert Cialdini, *Influence: The Science and Practice*, 4th ed. (Needham Heights, MA: Allyn and Bacon, 2005).

8. "Pop-up Retail" (trendwatching.com/trends/POPUP_RETAIL.htm), accessed October 19, 2015.

9. "Nike City Cup, Havas Sports & Entertainment" (www.havas-se.us/our-work/nike-city-cup), accessed October 26, 2015.

10. "Nike City Cup, POPSOP" (popsop.com/2011/06/nike-nike-city-cup/), accessed July 1, 2016.

11. "FedEx Kinkos 'No More All-Nighters' Campaign Awakens Interest in Online Tools,'" *Ad Age* (adage.com/article/btob/fedex-kinko-s-nighters-campaign-awakens-interest-online-tools/268039/), accessed October 26, 2015.

12. Ann-Christine Diaz, "Behind the Work: Volkswagen's 'The Fun Theory,' " *Ad Age* (adage.com/article/behind-the-work/work-volkswagen-s-fun-theory/139512/), accessed October 20, 2015.

13. The Fun Theory (www.thefuntheory.com), accessed October 20, 2015.

14. "Southwest Airlines Careers" (www.southwest.com/html/about-southwest/careers/), accessed October 19, 2015.

CHAPTER 10

1. "Sponsorship Spending Growth Slows in North America," IEGSR (www.sponsorship.com/iegsr/2014/01/07/Sponsorship-Spending-Growth-Slows-In-North-America.aspx), accessed October 31, 2015.

2. "Crystal Light to Host Mega Words With Friends Game," *Marketing Daily* (www.mediapost.com/publications/article/199910/crystal-light-to-host-mega-words-with-friends-game.html), accessed November 2, 2015.

3. "Reciprocal Loyalty—The Best Way to Acquire and Retain Customers," *Entrepreneur* (www.entrepreneur.com/article/238663), accessed June 28, 2016.

4. "The Need for: Belonging," Changing Minds (changingminds.org/explanations/needs/belonging.htm), accessed June 28, 2016.

5. "Plant a Seed: Frosted Flakes Super Bowl Commercial" (www.youtube.com/watch?v=UX0aTKuBNCI), accessed November 3, 2015.

6. Mac Presents, "Case Studies" (www.macpresents.com/programs), accessed June 15, 2016.

7. "The Happiness Flag," Association of National Advertisers (www.ana.net/miccontent/show/id/reggie-2015-cocacola), accessed October 29, 2015.

8. "10 Tic Tac x Minions Facts from Cannes Lions by Roman Olivarez," *Adobo* (www.adobomagazine.com/global-news/10-tic-tac-x-minions-facts-cannes-lions-roman-olivarez), accessed June 28, 2016.

9. "WWF and the Coca-Cola Company Team Up to Protect Polar Bears," World Wildlife Fund (www.worldwildlife.org/projects/wwf-and-the-coca-cola-company-team-up-to-protect-polar-bears).

10. "Droga 5's 'Decode Jay Z' for Bing Wins Again," *Ad Age* (adage.com/article/special-report-cannes-2011/cannes-decode-jay-z-wins-integrated-grand-prix/228429/), accessed June 28, 2016.

11. "Droga 5's 'Decode Jay Z' for Bing Wins Again," *Ad Age*.

CHAPTER 11

1. Jerry Swerling, Kjerstin Thorson, Burghardt Tenderich, Aimei Yang, Zongchao (Cathy) Li, Emily Gee, and Emily Savastano, "PR by the Numbers," Public Relations Society of America (media.prsa.org/pr-by-the-number/), accessed April 4, 2016.

2. Matt Johnson, "The Role of Brand Journalism in the Modern Marketing Mix," CMO (www.cmo.com/articles/2015/2/22/the_role_of_brand_jo.html), accessed April 4, 2016.

3. "The CMO's Guide to Brand Journalism," The Lyons Series, HubSpot (cdn2.hubspot.net/hub/53/file-562750272-pdf/Brand_Journalism_Guide_for_CMOs.pdf?utm_referrer=http%3A%2F%2Fwww.hubspot.com%2Fcmos-guide-to-brand-journalism), accessed February 29, 2016.

4. Private conversation with Claudia Strauss, January 5, 2016.

5. Personal correspondence with Claudia Strauss, April 15, 2016.

6. Personal communication with Claudia Strauss, January 12, 2016.

7. "Guns with History" Case Study (www.youtube.com/watch?v=nhkzXGqaWts), accessed March 14, 2016.

8. "The Gun Shop" Case Study (grey.com/global/work/key/new-york-gun-shop/id/5632/), accessed March 14, 2016.

9. Sean Corcoran, "Defining Earned, Owned, and Paid Media," Sean Corcoran's Blog, Forrester (blogs.forrester.com/interactive_marketing/2009/12/defining-earned-owned-and-paid-media.html), accessed October 31, 2015.

10. Richard Pinder, "The Consumer Doesn't Draw a Distinction between Advertising and PR—So Why Would We?," *The Drum* (www.thedrum.com/opinion/2016/02/23/consumer-doesn-t-draw-distinction-between-advertising-and-pr-so-why-would-we), accessed May 16, 2016.

11. Doug Gross, "Social Web Tackles the #Icebucketchallenge" (www.cnn.com/2014/08/13/tech/ice-bucket-challenge/index.html), accessed November 1, 2015.

12. "Pete Frates" (en.wikipedia.org/wiki/Pete_Frates), accessed November 2, 2015.

13. Gross, "Social Web Tackles the #Icebucketchallenge."

14. John Bonifield, "One Year Later, Your ALS Ice Bucket Money Goes To . . ." (www.cnn.com/2015/07/15/health/one-summer-after-the-als-ice-bucket-challenge/), accessed November 1, 2015.

15. Private conversation with Matt Carlson, March 27, 2016.

16. "When Is Bad Publicity Good," Stanford Graduate School of Business (www.gsb.stanford.edu/insights/when-bad-publicity-good), accessed April 10, 2016.

17. Gengi Cui, Hon-Kwong Lui, and Xiaoning Guo, "The Effect of Online Consumer Reviews on New Product Sales," *International Journal of Electronic Commerce* 17, no. 1 (Fall 2012): 39–57.

18. Sam Decker, "6 Reasons to Not Fear Negative Reviews," ClickZ (www.clickz.com/clickz/column/1725342/reasons-not-fear-negative-reviews), accessed May 16, 2016.

19. Vikki Chowney, "Bad Reviews Improve Conversion by 67%," Econsultancy (econsultancy.com/blog/8638-bad-reviews-improve-conversion-by-67/), accessed May 16, 2016.

20. Decker, "6 Reasons to Not Fear Negative Reviews."

21. "An American Comeback Story: Resurgent Brands and Great Products Tell the Story of the New GM: Silver Anvil 2011," PRSA (www.prsa.org/SearchResults/

view/6BE-1102C01/0/Resurgent_Brands_and_Great_Products_Tell_the_Story#
.VjlBJIRv938), accessed November 3, 2015.

22. "Arby's Smoking Hot Brisket Campaign Breaks Marketing Record with
Smokehouse Brisket Program," PRSA (www.prsa.org/SearchResults/view/6BE-
1502AE1970/0/Arby_s_Smoking_Hot_Brisket_Campaign_Breaks_Marketi#.
VjlA4IRv938), accessed November 3, 2015.

23. Matthew Rothenberg, "Oreo, the Oscars, and Real-Time Marketing:
How 'Dunk in the Dark' Helped and Harmed the Brand Newsroom" (contently.
com/strategist/2015/02/20/oreo-the-oscars-and-real-time-marketing-how-dunk-in-
the-dark-helped-and-harmed-the-brand-newsroom/), accessed November 2, 2015.

24. Ira Basen,"Breaking Down the Wall," University of Wisconsin Center for
Journalism Ethics (ethics.journalism.wisc.edu/2012/12/19/breaking-down-the-
wall/), accessed November 1, 2015.

25. "Brand Journalism vs. Content Marketing," Hook PR Group (hookpr.com/
brand-journalism-vs-content-marketing/), accessed November 6, 2015.

26. Rachael Post, "Introducing Investigative Brand Journalism" (www.linkedin.
com/pulse/introducing-investigative-brand-journalism-rachael-post?trk=hp-feed-
article-title-comment), accessed March 16, 2016.

CHAPTER 12

1. Opinion Research Corporation, June 2015.

2. Agency Research, October 2014.

3. KC GMRA, June–August 2015.

4. Facebook Insights, Twitter Analytics, YouTube Insights, June 15, 2015–August 31,
2015.

5. Millward Brown, August 2015.

Index

Illustrations are indicated by page references in *italics*.

About the Authors

William Rosen leads VSA Partners' marketing practice, overseeing advertising and marketing efforts for clients including ABInBev, Harley-Davidson, Nike, McDonald's, and Beam Suntory. Prior to beginning his engagement as a partner at VSA Partners, William was president and chief creative officer of North America for Arc Worldwide, the global marketing company, and part of Leo Burnett Worldwide and the Publicis Group. He led digital, direct/CRM, promotion, and shopper/retail marketing for clients including McDonald's, Procter & Gamble, Coca-Cola, Nestlé Purina, Comcast, Walgreens, United Airlines, Whirlpool, and MillerCoors.

Widely recognized as a leader in cross-channel marketing, William has been honored more than three hundred times with major creative awards and rankings around the world, including Best New Media, Best Multidiscipline Campaign, several Best in Show awards, and three Lions at the Cannes International Advertising Festival.

Since 2011, William's work for MillerCoors, Procter & Gamble, Symantec, Walgreens, Kimberly-Clark, and others has received fourteen Effie Awards, the industry's most prestigious prize for effectiveness. His work for Walgreens was honored with the MAA Worldwide Globes Best of the Best in the World, as well as the Oracle World Retail Award's Retail Advertising Campaign of the Year.

William served as president of the jury at the Cannes Lions International Advertising Festival, as well as the Spikes Asia Advertising Festival, and has served on juries for the Clio Awards, the Effie Awards, the London International Advertising Awards, and numerous other leading industry award shows.

Laurence Minsky is recognized in both professional and academic circles for his strategic and creative leadership and his broad-reaching industry experience as an educator, marketing strategist, creative director, copywriter, and consultant. His industry experience and expertise includes brand development, brand advertising, brand activation, content marketing, new product development, local store marketing, direct response, interactive, online and mobile marketing, and channel communications, as well as developing effective cross-channel solutions that boost marketing ROI.

He currently serves as an associate professor in the Department of Communication and Media Innovation of the School of Media Arts at Columbia College Chicago and as a consultant for leading agencies, corporations, and nonprofits across the globe.

Laurence is the executive editor of *The Get A Job Workshop: How to Find Your Way to a Creative Career in Advertising, Branding, Collateral, Digital, Experiential & More*; the author of *How to Succeed in Advertising When All You Have Is Talent* (second edition); and a coauthor of *Advertising and the Business of Brands* (Media Revolution edition). As an industry thought-leader, he has been published by the *Harvard Business Review*, Marketing-Profs, and the Data-Driven Marketing Network, and has been quoted in the *New York Times, Chicago Tribune, Chicago Sun-Times, San Diego Union Tribune, Exame* (Brazil's largest business and economics magazine), and *Crain's Chicago Business*, among many others.

His agency experience includes a tenure at Frankel (now Arc Worldwide) as well as engagements with more than twenty-five other agencies as a consultant. He has created marketing and communications solutions for many blue-chip clients, including Laila Ali, Ambius, Amazon, Bay Valley Foods, Beltone, Black & Decker Spacemaker, Bristol-Myers Squibb, Connie's Pizza, Fleetwood Homes, Frito-Lay, George Foreman Products, Lakeside Collection, Lamin-Art, Mayo Medical Laboratories, McDonald's, Midtown Athletic Clubs, Motorola, PetSmart, Sears, Spacelabs Healthcare, Taiwan External

Trade Development Council, United Airlines, United States Postal Service, Westinghouse, Vita Foods, and many more.

An award-winning creative with over 125 industry accolades to date, he has served on the juries of many leading industry award shows and is a long-standing member of the One Club for Art and Copy, the Authors Guild, and the American Academy of Advertising.